Praise for
THE ANATOMY OF DECONVERSION

"The importance of this topic cannot be overstated. Understanding why some believers risk it all to renounce their faith is crucial to helping those who struggle. This book is written with a pastoral goal in mind: help prevent deconversion. Its many accounts of falling away and recommitting will help readers develop the emotional competence to come alongside a struggler and help them fight for faith."

—**Steven H. Sanchez,** professor of Bible, The Moody Bible Institute

"Heartrending, hopeful, and pastorally wise. It is no secret that atheism is on the rise, even where Christianity is still the norm. John Marriott shares and analyzes real-life stories of Christians who have left the fold. He identifies problematic practices and teachings that correlate with deconversion, suggesting alternatives. Pastors, professors, and church leaders will want to read this so they can help foster resilient loyalty to Jesus the King."

—**Matthew W. Bates,** author of *Gospel Allegiance*, associate professor of theology, Quincy University

"In this carefully researched and thoughtful book, John Marriott listens to the voices of those who have left the faith, probes the factors leading to deconversion, and offers sensible and helpful suggestions for avoiding problems leading to loss of faith. Although the issues are certainly troubling, this is essential reading for pastors and Christian educators."

—**Harold Netland,** professor of Philosophy of Religion and Intercultural Studies, Trinity Evangelical Divinity School

"I recommend *The Anatomy of Deconversion* to anyone seeking to learn more about why deconversion happens and how crises of faith can become opportunities for discipleship instead of precursors to apostasy."

—**Bonnie Kristian,** author of *A Flexible Faith*, columnist at *Christianity Today*

"I cannot recommend this book enough. I know of no other book that gives such a thoughtful, insightful, and applicable approach to the topic of deconversion. It offers practical advice on avoiding and averting the possibility of deconversion and offers hope for those who have a loved one still in the struggle. You won't regret taking up this important work."

—**Richard S. Park,** assistant professor of Theology & Ethics, Vanguard University

"This book is unique because it is based on interviews with the deconverted. It is readable, practical, and hopeful. ... tical suggestions for how we can better prep ... bord

of ideas and challenges to the Christian faith that are now only one Google search away. I highly encourage you to buy several copies that you can share with other parents and your pastor to help us win this increasing challenge called deconversion."

—**Chris McGregor,** pastor, City Church, Montréal, Canada

"A must-read for anyone concerned about the rise of the religious 'nones' and specifically of those walking away from the Christian faith. Maintaining that deconversion is less about doctrine than about people, Marriott's insightful analysis of why and how people lose their faith is based on careful interviews of twenty-four former evangelicals or fundamentalists. Of special value is his discussion of the need for careful introspection both within the home and the church in what may contribute to this troubling trend."

—**Peter C. Hill,** Rosemead School of Psychology, Biola University, coauthor of *The Psychology of Fundamentalism*

"Drawing from personal accounts, psychological frameworks, and research data, Marriott provides a thoughtful, insightful analysis of reasons why many evangelical and fundamentalist Christians decide to leave the faith. He also carefully outlines both challenges and growth opportunities that may accompany such decisions. Finally, he suggests well-reasoned strategies that members of Christian communities might consider in the quest to help others keep, transform, or return to their faith."

—**Dr. Julie J. Exline,** professor, Department of Psychological Sciences, Case Western Reserve University

"Although many know former Christians, not all can claim to have systematically analyzed stories from a very broad range of such people. Correctly identifying the problem is the first step to solving it. This book does just that. The final chapters are thought-provoking, getting Christians to think seriously about how they should present their faith to others, and how they should build a lasting faith in their fellow believers. The chapters also instill hope in us who mourn and grief. Now that deconversion is a global phenomenon, this book is a must-read for church leaders in all parts of the world."

—**C. Harry Hui,** Social-Organizational Psychologist, honorary associate professor, University of Hong Kong

THE
ANATOMY
OF
DECONVERSION

THE
ANATOMY
OF
DECONVERSION

KEYS TO A LIFELONG FAITH IN A
CULTURE ABANDONING CHRISTIANITY

JOHN MARRIOTT

Abilene Christian University Press

THE ANATOMY OF DECONVERSION

Keys to a Lifelong Faith in a Culture Abandoning Christianity

ACU
PRESS

Copyright © 2020 by John Marriott

ISBN 978-1-68426-201-4

Printed in the United States of America

Cataloging-in-Publication Data is on file at the Library of Congress, Washington, DC.

Cover design by ThinkPen Design
Interior text design by Sandy Armstrong, Strong Design

For information, contact:
Abilene Christian University Press
ACU Box 29138
Abilene, Texas 79699

1-877-816-4455
www.acupressbooks.com

21 22 23 24 25 26 / 7 6 5 4 3 2 1

For Nancy, the love of my life.

CONTENTS

INTRODUCTION

Writing about faith loss is not something I find enjoyable, but it is something that I think is important. When I first began researching faith exit, I did so out of curiosity. One night in graduate school, I happened to stumble across a website that hosted hundreds of deconversion narratives. I read them with a sense of both fascination and dread. Although I was aware that sometimes believers leave the faith, I was clueless about just how many Christians with a background like mine had done so. Ever since that night, I have spent a considerable amount of time researching why and how individuals leave the Christian faith. What I have discovered is that, by all indications, the number of individuals leaving the faith is growing at troubling rates. While I am not claiming that the church in the United States is in the midst of a deconversion crisis, it is clear that, for various reasons, individuals are leaving the faith in increasing numbers. It is incumbent on pastors and church leaders to understand why this is happening in order to appropriately respond to it. Presently, however, there exists very little analysis of faith exit among those who once identified as evangelical Christians and who now identify as nonbelievers of one sort or another. This book seeks to fill the gap that exists in the literature by providing an inside look at deconversion from the perspectives of those who have left the faith. What follows is the result of conducting numerous interviews with and reading hundreds of narratives by former Christians about why they left their faith, what the deconversion process was like, the circumstances that served as the context of their loss of faith, and the impact that deconverting has had on them, both negatively and positively.

The book is divided into three main sections. The first section addresses important philosophical and theological matters pertaining to deconversion. The focus is on discussing questions such as what constitutes deconversion, what a Christian is, what it means to believe, what the gospel is, and whether a genuine Christian can commit apostasy. This section provides a necessary foundation for the rest of the book. Without having a handle on the relevant biblical material, we will not be able to form an appropriate strategy of response. One issue in particular that this section addresses is whether a truly born-again believer in Jesus can commit apostasy. Theologically informed Christians hold differing views on this. Regardless, I'm confident that the discoveries of this study are applicable to whichever theological position one affirms. That is to say, for my purposes of this book, it's irrelevant whether one believes in the perseverance of the saints or that salvation can be lost. The insights offered throughout the book on deconversion and the suggestions for averting it are applicable to whichever theological camp one is in.

The second section of the book examines the reasons, process, background conditions, strategies, and impact of deconverting. It is divided into eight chapters, each dedicated to one topic and grounded in the testimony of those who have left the faith.

Chapter Three provides a look at the main reasons that are cited by former believers for why they left the faith.

Chapter Four gives insight into the process of deconversion. In essence, it addresses the question, "What does the losing of faith look like?" This will be fleshed out by answering a series of sub-questions, including: How does deconverting from a faith compare with the process of converting to a faith? What are the stages of the deconversion process? What is the point of no return?

Chapter Five unpacks the religious background of participants. Several themes that emerged from personal interviews and online deconversion "testimonies" combine to reveal important aspects of the lives of former Christians. These themes reveal much about what often underwrites the loss of faith. Furthermore, these themes raise important questions about what former believers have deconverted from.

Chapters Six and Seven reveal the many negative consequences that go along with faith exit. These range from the personal and social to the financial and vocational. Surprisingly, however, we will discover in Chapter Nine that, regardless of the negative consequences of losing their faith, the positive consequences were so meaningful that they made the negative consequences worth enduring. In Chapter Eight, the strategies employed by former believers in navigating the deconversion process are brought to the fore. This information is helpful in that it helps shed light on how former Christians go about forming new identities as unbelievers. As mentioned above, Chapter Nine addresses the positive impact of deconversion. It may come as a surprise to readers that former believers, for all of the negative consequences they endured as a result of losing their faith, uniformly testify that it was worth it for what they received in return. Again, this raises the question of what it was that believers deconverted from. How could someone know and walk with the Lord Jesus, who promised his followers a yoke that was easy and a burden that was light, come to the place where they were willing to lose almost everything to be set free from him?

The third and final section of the book, Chapters Eleven, Twelve, and Thirteen, shifts from a descriptive posture to a prescriptive one. Here, we will explore three things. First, we will discuss how we can avoid setting up believers under our care for an unnecessary crisis of faith. Believe it or not, well-intentioned pastors and parents can and do place stumbling blocks to faith before believers; the more sensitive we are to what those are, the less likely we will be to do so. Second, we will consider practical ways that we can avert the shipwreck of faith by walking with those who are struggling to maintain their commitment to Christ. Third, we will look at ways to cultivate a lasting faith by providing believers with a strong foundation upon which they can build their faith. It is my hope that, in doing so, we will be able to help believers construct a faith that endures, as opposed to one that will not.

I end the book in Chapter Thirteen with stories of hope. It is important to do so because too often, parents, spouses, and siblings can feel despondent when a loved one leaves the faith because they feel all is lost. However, that is not true. Although the stories of reconversions are not as voluminous online, they exist and are growing. These stories provide hope that just because a person walks away from their faith at one time in their life does not mean that they will continue to walk in that same direction. Sometimes they make U-turns. Knowing this can make all the difference in the world for friends and families of deconverts.

PART 1

THEOLOGICAL ISSUES

CHAPTER ONE

DECONVERSION: THE BODY OF EVIDENCE

Set for the Defense of the Gospel

At age eighteen, John Loftus made a decision to follow Jesus, and that decision radically changed his life. He notes that his conversion was so sweeping that there was "no one who knew me during my early years as a Christian who would say I was not on fire for God. I burned with a passion for the Lord. And for good reason; I believed God turned my life around."[1] A problem teenager who was kicked out of his high school several times, Loftus would go on to be arrested six times as a juvenile offender. As many often do in his situation, he turned to God for help. Assuming it was God's Word, he began reading the Bible and believed everything he read. He accepted Jesus as his savior and quickly got involved in a church youth group. To say that he was passionate about his faith would be an understatement. He went witnessing every weekend in the downtown core of his hometown of Fort Wayne, Indiana, including outside of a "couple strip joints and one gay bar."[2] He would even go hitchhiking with the "express purpose" of witnessing

---

[1] John Loftus, *The Christian Delusion: Why Faith Fails* (Amherst, NY: Prometheus Books, 2010).

[2] Loftus, *Christian Delusion*, 21.

to whoever picked him up.[3] In his words, he "witnessed to everyone almost all the time."[4]

But Loftus wasn't just all heat and no light. He was also passionate to learn about the faith that he so enthusiastically shared with others. He devoured Josh and Sean McDowell's popular apologetics book, *Evidence That Demands a Verdict*, and many of Francis Schaeffer's more philosophical apologetic works. The result of his research was an overwhelming confidence that the Christian faith "could handle the attacks of all the critics" because he concluded that it was clear: "Christianity is true!"[5] Loftus eventually enrolled in a Midwest Bible college, where he gained a working knowledge of Scripture. After graduating, he took a position as an associate pastor at a church in Kalkaska, Michigan. Concurrently, he enrolled in and then graduated from an evangelical seminary with master's degrees in theology and divinity. While in seminary, Loftus founded and edited the now defunct *Apologetics Quarterly: A Journal for Christian Studies*. In 1985, Loftus attended Trinity Evangelical Divinity School, studied under noted apologist William Lane Craig, and earned a master's degree in theology. After graduation, he became the senior pastor at Angola Christian Church in Angola, Indiana. In Loftus's own words, he "was a Christian apologist with several master's degrees set for the express purpose of defending Christianity from intellectual attacks."[6]

Today, Loftus is one of America's foremost apologists—not for Christianity, however, but for atheism. No longer is he writing on behalf of Christianity but, rather, against it. Instead of witnessing on behalf of Christ, he is debating believers about the foolishness of being a Christian. Rather than editing an apologetics journal, he is editing a website that is intended to debunk Christianity. For various reasons, some intellectual, some personal, and some interpersonal, he came to

---

[3] Loftus, *Christian Delusion*, 21.
[4] Loftus, *Christian Delusion*, 21.
[5] Loftus, *Christian Delusion*, 21.
[6] Loftus, *Christian Delusion*, 13.

the place, like many others, where he no longer believed in Jesus. He deconverted, and he now eagerly works to deconvert others.

If you are reading this book, it is likely that you know someone who, like John Loftus, left the faith. Likely, you are trying to understand how it is that someone who once believed the claims of the Bible, who was involved in a church, and who happily identified as a follower of Jesus could possibly walk away from it all. Perhaps they were in your youth group, congregation, or even family. And while the individuals you know who have left the faith may not have a story that is as dramatic as John Loftus's, it is likely no less confusing and discouraging. Sadly, John Loftus and those you may know who have left the faith are not a small group of outliers. Surveys and studies indicate that a growing number of Christians are leaving not only the church as an institution but also Christianity itself.

By the Numbers

Among websites advocating atheism on the Internet, there exists a large number dedicated to cataloging deconversion stories of former Christians who now identify as atheists. This may surprise you, but these testimonies number in the tens of thousands and are increasing. Moreover, the testimonies range from those new to the faith and those who leave it soon after, including former pastors, former missionaries, and former seminary professors.

In the United States, the number of individuals who identify as having no religion is growing significantly.[7] The "nones," as they are referred to, don't identify with any religion. They may be agnostics, atheists, or merely individuals who do not subscribe to any particular religious faith. For some, the lack of religious affiliation is the result of being raised in

---

[7] A 2014 Pew survey reported that 22.8 percent of the population identified as having no religious affiliation, up from 16.1 percent in 2007. Among respondents, 33 percent said they do not believe in God, and nearly 40 percent said that religion has no importance to them at all. Between 2007 and 2014, the percentage of those who identified as atheists nearly doubled, while the number of Christians dropped 7.8 percent (Protestants, Catholics, and mainline). www.pewforum.org/2015/05/12/americas-changing-religious-landscape/.

homes without any religious commitments. For others, however, it's due to a conscious decision to leave the religion they once adhered to. It's interesting to note that as the number of nones goes up, the numbers of Christians decreases. In fact, those once committed to following Jesus are deconverting in record numbers and at record rates.[8] In a 2015 CNN article, Greg Smith, associate director of religion research at the Pew Research Center, said, "We've known that the religiously unaffiliated has been growing for decades. But the pace at which they've continued to grow is really astounding."[9] Let me give you a whistle-stop tour of the statistics as they relate to faith exit over the last eighteen years.

In 2002, the Southern Baptist Convention (SBC) reported that it was losing 88 percent of its youth after their freshman year in college.[10] At the same time, 70 percent of SBC teenagers involved in church youth groups stopped attending church within two years of their high school graduation.[11] The Barna Group announced in 2006 that 61 percent of young adults who were involved in church during their teen years had become spiritually disengaged.[12] Supporting Barna's findings, a 2007 Assemblies of God study reported that between 50 percent and 67 percent of Assemblies of God young people who attend a non-Christian public or private university will have left the faith four years after entering college.[13] A similar study from LifeWay Research that came out the same year claimed that 70 percent of students lose their faith in college, and of those, only 35 percent eventually return to their faith.[14]

---

[8] Drew Dyck, *Generation Ex-Christian: Why Young Adults Are Leaving the Faith and How to Bring Them Back* (Chicago: Moody Press, 2010)

[9] Daniel Burke, "Millennials Leaving Church in Droves, Study Finds," *CNN*, May 14, 2015.

[10] Jon Walker, "Family Life Council Says It's Time to Bring Family Back to Life," *Baptist Press*, SBC Annual Meeting, June 12, 2002.

[11] T. C. Pinckney, "We Are Losing Our Children," remarks to the Southern Baptist Convention Executive Committee, September 18, 2001.

[12] "Most Twentysomethings Put Christianity on the Shelf Following Spiritually Active Teen Years," Barna Group, September 11, 2006.

[13] Dayton Kingsriter, "Is the Lower Cost Worth the Higher Price?" General Council of the Assemblies of God, 2007, https://silo.tips/download/is-the-lower-cost-worth -the-high-price.

[14] "Reasons 18- to 22-Year-Olds Drop Out of Church," LifeWay Research, August 7, 2007.

In May 2009, the Pew Research Center's Forum on Religion and Public Life presented research claiming that young Americans are leaving religion at five to six times the historic rate. They also noted that the percentage of young Americans who identify as having no religion is between 30 and 40 percent, up from 5–10 percent only a generation ago.[15] That same year, the Fuller Youth Institute's study, the College Transition Project, discovered that current data seems "to suggest that about 40–50 percent of students in youth groups struggle in their faith after graduation."[16]

A 2003 UCLA study titled "Spirituality in Higher Education" found that only 29 percent of college students regularly attended church after their junior year, down from 52 percent the year before they entered college.[17] A second UCLA study, "The College Student Survey," asked students to indicate their present religious commitment. Researchers then compared the responses of freshmen who checked the "born again" category with the answers they gave four years later when they were seniors. What they found was shocking. On some campuses, as much as 59 percent of students no longer described themselves as "born again."[18]

Given what we know regarding the loss of faith among American young people, it will come as no surprise that the class of 2018 in the United States cares less about their religious identity than any previous college freshmen class in the last forty years. A third study by UCLA found that students across the United States are dissociating themselves from religion in record numbers. "The American Freshman" study reveals that nearly 28 percent of the 2014 incoming college freshmen did not identify with any religious faith. That is a sharp increase from 1971, when only 16 percent of freshmen said they did not identify

---

[15] Dyck, *Generation Ex-Christian*.

[16] "Sticky College Campuses," Fuller Youth Institute, December 12, 2011.

[17] Kevin Bonderud and Michael Fleischer, "College Students Show High Levels of Spiritual and Religious Engagement," Higher Education Research Institute, UCLA, November 21, 2003.

[18] J. H. Pryor, Sylvia Hurtado, Victor B. Saenz, José Luis Santos, and William S. Korn, "The American Freshman: Forty Year Trends," Higher Education Research Institute, April 2007.

with a specific religion.[19] In 2015, the Pew Research Center conducted a study titled "Choosing a New Church or House of Worship," in which researchers asked participants to identify the criteria by which they choose their place of worship. Interestingly, the survey revealed, "Roughly eight-in-ten religious 'nones' say they were raised with a religious affiliation."[20] This means that nearly 80 percent of "nones" surveyed were at one time in a faith community before jettisoning it. In a 2016 survey, ominously titled "Exodus: Why Americans Are Leaving Religion—and Why They're Unlikely to Come Back," researchers at the Public Religion Research Institute concluded that nearly 40 percent of young adults age 18–29 are religiously unaffiliated.[21] That is nearly four times as likely among young adults only one generation ago. More troubling is the finding that 79 percent of young adults age 18–29 who leave the faith and identify as nones do so during their teenage years. Those of previous generations did so much later. For example, those over sixty-five years of age who left their faith during their teen years numbered only 38 percent. The stunning takeaway of the report is as follows: "Today, one-quarter (25 percent) of Americans claim no formal religious identity, *making this group the single largest 'religious group in the U.S.'*"[22] Finally, the 2019 General Social Survey discovered that Americans with "no religion" now account for about 23.1 percent of the population. That is up from 21.6 percent just three years earlier. Over that same period, American individuals identifying as evangelicals dropped slightly from 23.9 percent to 22.5 percent. Statistically, this means that the two groups are tied.

More studies could have been included, but I trust they are not needed. It is indisputable—nonbelief in the United States is on the rise,

---

[19] Kevin Eagan, Ellen Bara Stolzenberg, Joseph J. Ramirez, Milissa C. Aragon, Maria Ramirez Suchard, and Sylvia Hurtado, "The American Freshman: National Norms Fall 2014," Higher Education Research Institute at UCLA, 2014.

[20] "Choosing a New Church or House of Worship," Pew Research Center Religion & Public Life, August 23, 2016.

[21] Betsy Cooper, Daniel Cox, Rachel Lienesch, and Robert P. Jones, "Exodus: Why Americans Are Leaving Religion—and Why They're Unlikely to Come Back," Public Religion Research Institute, September 22, 2016.

[22] Cooper et al., "Exodus," emphasis mine.

and part of that is because the number of Christians leaving their faith is increasing. At present, there are no signs of this trend slowing down. Deconversion is on the rise, but just what is deconversion?[23]

Defining Deconversion

Not everyone who identifies as a none or who is religiously unaffiliated is a deconvert, but all deconverts, as I am using the term, are religious nones. By that, I mean that some religious nones never identified as a member of a religious community to begin with, so they had nothing to deconvert from. In other words, it's conceivable that not a few religious nones were raised in homes that never identified with a particular religious tradition. Deconverts, on the other hand, at one time identified as believers and were part of religious communities, only to renounce those beliefs and their membership in those communities. How much of the rise of the nones is the result of deconversions from Christianity is hard to calculate, but according to one commentator, the "vast majority" of the nones "are ex-Christians, and most are under the age of 35."[24] On top of that, for every convert to Christianity, there are four deconverts from Christianity who identify as religious nones.[25] What this tells us is that a good number of religious nones are not individuals who were raised in secular homes or inevitably drifted away from a nominal faith that they were only weakly attached to. Many nones are deconverts—those who have evaluated the Christian faith, found it to be wanting, and deconverted from it. These individuals are the focus of this book.

Deconversion is a type of religious transition. The process has been identified by a handful of different terms. Some of the more common terms are *dropping out*, *apostasy*, *faith exit*, and *religious disaffiliation*. Although the essence of what constitutes deconversion is fuzzy,

---

[23] This section, "By the Numbers," is used by permission of Wipf and Stock Publishers. www.wipfandstock.com.

[24] J. Warner Wallace, "Young Christians Are Leaving the Church—Here's Why," *Fox News*, September 9, 2018.

[25] Cathy Lynn Grossman, "Christians Drop, 'Nones' Soar in New Religion Portrait," *USA Today*, May 12, 2015.

there is enough overlap among the terms to make sense of what they mean. In each case, they involve the rejection of religious beliefs and disengagement from a religious community. In this book, the term *deconversion* refers to the rejection of Christian beliefs, disengagement from a Christian community, and having no religious affiliation.

Some might wonder if adding "none" to the definition confuses two different religious transitions: "deconversion from" and "conversion to." The short answer is no, it doesn't. While there is some truth to the claim that "every conversion to one position is a deconversion from another," deconversion from a faith tradition to none is not the same as conversion. That's because there are a number of differences that characterize transitioning from a faith tradition and becoming a none that are quite different from converting to a faith tradition and becoming a believer. For example, conversion to a faith tradition nearly always includes adopting a comprehensive set of doctrines and becoming embedded in a religious community. That is not the case when one becomes a none, which lacks a comprehensive set of doctrines and an identifiable community.[26] Likewise, conversion to a religious faith is usually accompanied by both a sense of choice and a sense of great gain. Believers choose to become Christians—it is an act of the will, a commitment to a faith system that provides them with great spiritual gain. Not so with deconversion. Deconverts generally do not choose to leave their faith but find themselves having lost their faith. When this happens, it is not often immediately accompanied by a sense of gain, but of deep loss, both personally and socially.[27] There are more differences between deconversion and conversion, but for now, I trust that the point has been made. Deconversion is its own unique experience.

Anatomy Lesson

I remember in high school dissecting frogs in biology class. The purpose of the assignment was to learn about the anatomy of reptiles. We

---

[26] Lori Fazzino, "Leaving the Church Behind: Applying a Deconversion Perspective to Evangelical Exit Narratives," *Journal of Contemporary Religion* 29, no. 2 (2014): 249–66.

[27] More will be said below about the positive impact of losing faith.

would identify and then cut out the various organs, muscles, and skeletal parts of the frog and pin them to a tray with prefixed labels. It was both interesting and disgusting at the same time. Little did I know at the time that, in doing my dissection, I stood in a long line of scientists interested in understanding the anatomy of living things. The study of anatomy goes as far back as at least ancient Greece. Born in 335 BC, Herophilus of Chalcedon is often credited as the father of ancient anatomical study. He is one of the first people, if not the first, to complete systematic dissections for the purpose of understanding the makeup of the human body. He also carried out autopsies in order to chart the course of disease. His research shed new and important light on the brain, the eye, the reproductive organs, and the nervous system.

But Herophilus's work, as important as it was, didn't provide a comprehensive account of human anatomy. It moved the needle forward, but a complete picture of human anatomy was still lacking. That is until Andreas Vesalius came along. Vesalius, born in 1514 in Brussels, Belgium, began his academic career studying the humanities, but he eventually changed course and studied medicine at the University of Paris. It was there where he became enamored with human anatomy. Upon graduation and taking up a teaching position, Vesalius revolutionized the study of anatomy. Until that time, anatomy was taught primarily by studying the classical texts of ancient authors. Vesalius, however, was more hands-on. His preferred method was to have students dissect cadavers themselves. In 1543, he published his groundbreaking work, *On the Fabric of the Human Body*. It was the first comprehensive anatomical text based on the findings of firsthand accounts and illustrations of dissections. It even included three-dimensional models of organs. Vesalius had produced the first comprehensive anatomical account of the human body. His account was not the last word on the subject. There was much more to be discovered, and those who followed in his footsteps have done just that.

The study of deconversion can be compared to the state of affairs when Herophilus wrote his works on anatomy. Just as he studied important anatomical aspects of the human body and provided insight on them, so too have researchers provided some insight on the whys and hows of deconversion. But like Herophilus, they have yet to produce a comprehensive account of the subject as a whole. What is needed is a work along the lines of Vesalius, a comprehensive account of deconversion, not just studies on its various parts. While I make no claims to be the Vesalius of deconversion, the book you hold in your hands is my attempt to provide a more comprehensive account of deconversion than has previously existed. It is not a study on one aspect of the loss of faith, but an anatomy of deconversions as a whole.

Says Who?

The best way to discover the whys and hows of deconversion is to ask former Christians to share their stories. So, for several years, that's just what I did. I conducted in-depth interviews with individuals that shed light on the nature of their deconversions. In doing so, I gained insight as to why they lost their faith, the process of losing their faith, strategies that they used to mitigate the negative consequences of deconversion, and the various contexts within which their deconversions took place.

I interviewed roughly an equal number of men and women from across the United States. Their ages ranged from early twenties to midfifties, and all had identified as Christian for varying lengths of time. Some were believers for only a few years; others were for several decades. Each held beliefs that placed them within the broad scope of evangelical Christianity, which I define as including a conversion experience, a high view of the Bible as God's Word, a belief that salvation is mediated only through Jesus, and the belief that sharing the gospel is important. The group included a former seminary student, former pastors, a former church council member, a former worship leader, a former church intern, and former amateur apologists. The journey to unbelief for some was quick, almost instantaneous, while for others it took a number of years. Some experienced emotional difficulties as they let go of their faith, but most found it easy.

In order to understand and provide a robust portrait of deconversion, I had to first identify criteria by which I could identify former believers. There are many different sets of criteria that I could have chosen, but I settled on the following:

1. They had to have made a personal decision to follow Jesus Christ at one time.
2. They had to have been a member of an evangelical or fundamentalist church.
3. They had to have defected both institutionally and ideologically from Christianity. By this, I mean they must no longer accept that the fundamental beliefs of Christianity are true, and they must no longer attend a church.
4. They must identify as an unbeliever, which means they no longer affirm the claim that Christianity is true.

The individuals who met the criteria came from evangelical and fundamentalist church backgrounds from across the country and from varying degrees of conservatism, both in doctrine and in practice. For the purpose of this book, conservative evangelicals are the least conservative in doctrine and practice, compared to the other two (fundamentalists and hybrids of conservative evangelicalism and fundamentalism). Conservative evangelicals are primarily conservative when it comes to what they believe regarding the essentials of the faith. They are conservative in that they affirm the traditional doctrines of the historic Christian faith. Conservative evangelicals, at their best, tend to espouse an attitude of charity to other believers who differ on secondary and tertiary issues, but they stand firm on what they believe to be the essential teachings of the Bible. Typically, conservative evangelicals are ideologically to the right of popular culture when it comes to controversial social issues such as gender roles, the definition of marriage, and the legalization of marijuana. Practically speaking, conservative evangelicals espouse a mild separation from what is often called "the world," the system of thought and behavior that is out of sync with the teachings of the Bible and exemplified in the fashions of the current age. But conservative evangelicals are more accepting of consuming alcohol, going to movies, and styles of dress than their fundamentalist cousins. They seek to build bridges with the surrounding culture in order to reach it, and they are not afraid of incorporating various pragmatic means to do so.

At the opposite end of the spectrum are the fundamentalists. Fundamentalism arose in the early part of the twentieth century in response to challenges aimed at both the existence of God and the trustworthiness of the Bible. Characterized as a reactionary movement, theologian Roger Olson defines fundamentalism as follows:

> The distinctive hallmarks of post-1925 fundamentalism are (1) adding to those essentials of Christianity non-essentials such as premillennial eschatology, (2) "biblical separation" as the duty of every Christian to refuse fellowship with people who call themselves Christians but are considered doctrinally or morally impure, (3) a chronically negative and critical attitude toward culture including non-fundamentalist higher education, (4) emphatic anti-evolution, anti-communist, anti-Catholic and anti-ecumenical attitudes and actions (including elevation of young earth creationism and American exceptionalism as markers of authentic Christianity), (5) emphasis on verbal inspiration and technical inerrancy of the Bible as necessary for real Christianity (including exclusion of all biblical criticism and, often, exclusive use of the KJV), and (6) a general tendency to require adherence to traditional lifestyle norms (hair, clothes, entertainment, sex roles, etc.).[28]

The third group that emerged from the interviews was a hybrid of the conservative evangelicals and the fundamentalists. Some of the former Christians who shared their stories with me had church experiences that were evangelically conservative but had fundamentalist tendencies. This third group was predominantly characterized by the traits of conservative evangelicals with various strains of fundamentalism detectable in their stories.

---

[28] Roger Olson, "What Distinguishes Evangelical from Fundamentalist?" *My Evangelical Arminian Theological Musings* (blog), April 19, 2012.

Table 1.1 identifies the age, gender, location, and church typology of each participant.

Table 1.1

Participant Demographics

Name	Age	Gender	Location	Church
Anne	30–35	Female	Las Vegas, NV	CEF
Charlene	40–45	Female	Richmond, VA	CEF
Christopher	30–35	Male	Fullerton, CA	CEF
Cindy	45–50	Female	Simi Valley, CA	CEF
Dale	30–35	Male	Seattle, WA	CE
Dave	30–35	Male	Garland, TX	F
Derek	30–35	Male	Fort Smith, AK	F
Donald	25–30	Male	Walnut, CA	CE
Douglas	40–45	Male	San Francisco, CA	CE
Frank	40–45	Male	Grove City, PA	CE
Jill	40–45	Female	San Francisco, CA	CE
Kristen	35–40	Female	Seattle, WA	CEF
Kyle	25–30	Male	Irvine, CA	CE
Lauren	35–40	Female	Las Vegas, NV	CE
Marcus	20–25	Male	Los Angeles, CA	CE
Martin	40–45	Male	Las Vegas, NV	CEF
Mitch	20–25	Male	Irvine, CA	CEF
Rachel	50–55	Female	Durango, CO	F
Sam	50–55	Male	Durango, CO	CEF
Steve	25–30	Male	Nashville, TN	F
Shelley	45–50	Female	Seattle, WA	CEF
Tim	50–55	Male	Fargo, ND	F
Trina	40–45	Female	Los Angeles, CA	F
Wayne	35–40	Male	Houston, TX	CE

Legend: CEF = conservative evangelical with fundamentalist tendencies, F = fundamentalist, CE = conservative evangelical

Since writing my doctoral dissertation on the subject of deconversion, I have read hundreds of deconversion "testimonies" and have continued to engage in both the academic study of faith exit and informal discussions with former believers.[29] As I have done so, my understanding has grown. I now have a better insight into the major reasons why people lose their faith, what the deconversion process is, what experiences set up believers for a crisis of faith, and what the impact of deconverting is. As a result, I have come to the conclusion that there is good reason to hope that we can avert the kind of crisis that often leads to the loss of faith. Preventing deconversion isn't simply a matter of having good answers to hard questions, nor is it the result of doing church the "right" way. It is more complicated than that, but it is possible. In this book, my goals are to

- Provide you with a comprehensive understanding of the reasons, process, background conditions, and impact of deconversion
- Offer you insights on how we can avoid setting up believers for a crisis of faith that can lead to a loss of faith
- Provide suggestions on how to come alongside those in the throes of a serious faith crisis and how to provide them with helpful guidance in order to avert spiritual disaster

The Way Ahead

I invite you to keep reading and investigating the anatomy of deconversion. Join me in thinking about a daunting challenge that everyone in ministry will eventually have to face. In doing so, I believe you will come away with a greater understanding of the phenomenon, become aware of the mistakes made by well-meaning Christians that often set up believers for a crisis of faith, and become better equipped to help those who are clinging to faith.

---

[29] John Marriott, *A Recipe for Disaster: Four Ways Churches and Parents Prepare Individuals to Lose Their Faith and How They Can Instill a Faith That Endures* (Eugene, OR: Wipf & Stock, 2018).

CHAPTER TWO

IMPORTANT ISSUES

I Kissed Jesus Goodbye

In 1997, Joshua Harris burst onto the evangelical scene with his best-selling book on the benefits of courtship, titled *I Kissed Dating Goodbye*. Written when he was only twenty-one, the book went on to become a smash hit, eventually selling over one million copies. The publishing of *I Kissed Dating Goodbye* signaled an evangelical pushback to the sexually loose dating culture of the 1990s. Harris essentially called for a radical change in the way that Christians engage in relationships with the opposite sex. His book represented the rejection of the dominant cultural model through which young people entered into romantic relationships.[1]

Harris followed his initial publishing success with several more titles, including *Why Church Matters: Discovering Your Place in the Family of God, Stop Dating the Church! Fall in Love with the Family of God, Humble Orthodoxy: Holding the Truth High Without Putting People Down,* and *Dug Down Deep: Unearthing What I Believe and Why It Matters.* He became a widely sought-after conference speaker across

---

[1] Albert Mohler, "The Tragedy of Joshua Harris: Sobering Thoughts for Evangelicals," *Albert Mohler* (blog), August 1, 2019.

the United States, established his own series of conferences called New Attitude, and served as the senior pastor of a theologically conservative megachurch in Washington, DC. He was, without question, a high-profile leader in the evangelical world, until he wasn't.

In summer 2019, he shocked the Christian world by not only denouncing his books and announcing his divorce from his wife, but also pronouncing that he was no longer a Christian. In an Instagram post of him looking out over a blue-green lake surrounded by a majestic mountain, he stated, "I have undergone a massive shift in regard to my faith in Jesus. The popular phrase for this is 'deconstruction,' the biblical phrase is 'falling away.' By all the measurements that I have for defining a Christian, I am not a Christian."[2] And although he was appreciative of the prayers of those with whom he once identified, he wanted them to know that he was not wallowing in despair over any of his recent changes and that he was happy and optimistic about what lay ahead. The post read, "I can't join in your mourning. I don't view this moment negatively. I feel very much alive, and awake, and surprisingly hopeful."[3]

The next week, the man who was the evangelical advocate for courtship and a traditional view of biblical sexuality and marriage marched in an LGBTQ pride parade. Needless to say, the shock waves from Harris's deconversion have reverberated throughout the evangelical church. Joshua Harris's deconversion devastated not only those close to him and those in his church, but all those who looked up to him as a leader in the evangelical movement. Referring to Harris's apostasy, one prominent evangelical wrote, "It's hard to imagine more sobering news."[4]

While Joshua Harris's story is still being written, it certainly has taken a tragic and deeply discouraging turn. Sadly, however, his story is far from unique. His story is only exceptional because he had such a high profile, which, in turn, has resulted in such a large fall-out. Otherwise, Harris is but one more example of the thousands of

---

[2] Joshua Harris (Harrisjosh), "My Heart Is Full of Gratitude," Instagram, July 26, 2019, www.instagram.com/p/BoZBrNLH2sl/.

[3] Harris, "My Heart Is Full."

[4] Mohler, "Tragedy of Joshua Harris."

individuals who have deconverted from the faith and now identify as religious nones. The number of former believers who have exited the faith is stunning. There is, at present, a silent exodus from the faith occurring among evangelicals in the United States and Canada. A simple Internet search produced nearly fifty websites dedicated to deconversion and containing thousands of testimonies of those who once identified as Christians, only to have left the faith behind. Sources range from those who once were in ministry, such as pastors, ministers, and missionaries, to those who filled the pews on Sundays. There are specific websites for former believers of nearly every denomination that you can think of, as well as dozens of sites intended to help those who are in the process of leaving their faith. Clearly, Joshua Harris is not alone in walking away.

Joshua Harris's deconversion raises difficult questions that need answers. Two of the most urgent questions being asked by Christians are: How could such a thing happen to someone who seemed so solid and was such a role model of Christian commitment? What is there, if anything, that can be done to stop this from happening to those they love? We'll get to these questions shortly, but before we do, there are some preliminary questions that need to be addressed. I think it's helpful for readers to know how I answer the following questions since each one is relevant to the subject of deconversion. Specifically, there are three:

1. What is a Christian?
2. What is the gospel?
3. Can a genuine Christian commit apostasy?

What Is a Christian?

Can a Christian really lose their faith? Well, it all depends. What do you mean by Christian? In a book about deconverting from the Christian faith, I can think of no more important question to address at the start: What does this book assume about what it means to be a Christian? Not doing so can lead to potential misunderstandings and miscommunication. In order to avoid those pitfalls, I'll endeavor to be clear about what I mean when I use the term *Christian* throughout the book.

In the United States today, a majority of people continue to identify as Christian. And yet it is highly doubtful that the majority of those who say they are Christians actually are members of God's family. I assume that most people reading this book would agree with me in that assessment. But in saying that, however, I am assuming that the word *Christian* means something specific. There are at least two different meanings of the word *Christian* that are relevant to our discussion. The first is how the Bible uses the term, which is to identify an individual who has undergone a spiritual transformation by the work of the Spirit based on their faith in Christ. The second is how social scientists use the term, which is to identify those who self-label with the Christian faith but have not necessarily experienced a spiritual transformation. Both play an important role in the discussion of faith exit, but it is important that they be distinguished.

Clarifying Terms

Despite the fact that, today, the most common label for a follower of Jesus is "Christian," the Bible does not refer to Jesus's followers as Christians very often. The term occurs only three times in the Bible: Acts 11:26, Acts 26:28, and 1 Peter 4:16. But regardless of whether the authors of the New Testament call followers of Jesus "Christians," "believers," "saints," "disciples," or any other label, the inspired writers assume that, because of Jesus, such individuals have had a spiritual experience that has transformed them at the deepest level, that of their very nature. Biblically speaking, a Christian is a person who has experienced an ontological alteration at the most profound level of their being due to their belief in Christ, which, in turn, has brought them into a spiritual union with God. The Bible describes such persons as being reconciled with God, justified before God, redeemed by God, sanctified by God, and indwelt by the very Spirit of God. Because this change is spiritual in nature, it can't be detected by the senses, and thus it is not subject to empirical verification. However, the evidence of such a change can and should be detected if the change has really occurred. It's possible that a regenerated believer shows little evidence or even conceivably no evidence of salvation for long periods of time. But if there is never any evidence that accompanies a profession of faith, the New Testament indicates that the decisive ontological change has not taken place and that the person is not a Christian, biblically speaking.

When I use the term *evidence*, I'm using it to refer to what John the Baptist called the fruit of repentance. The fruit of repentance spoken of by John the Baptist is the action of bringing oneself into alignment with the rule and reign of God in one's life. Of course, no one does so perfectly. But without the rule and reign of God being manifest to some degree, it's highly questionable whether an individual is a Christian, biblically speaking.

It is important to point out, however—and this is extremely relevant to the subject of deconversion—that as important as the fruit of repentance is, the appearance of such fruit isn't a guarantee that a deep spiritual change has taken place in the life of someone who professes to be a follower of Jesus. Jesus himself makes this clear in the Gospel of Matthew, where he speaks about the future day of judgment when individuals offer him evidence that they are his followers and, as such, should be welcomed by him into his kingdom. On the surface, the evidence is impressive: prophesying in Jesus's name, casting out demons, and doing many mighty works. But Jesus will have none of it, and he tells them that he never knew them and that they must depart from him.[5] Why? Because although their lives showed evidence of what looked to be authentic fruit, in reality, it wasn't. Spectacular displays of power and authority do not necessarily prove that one is a genuine follower of Jesus, especially when they are not accompanied by a life intentionally lived according to the will of God.[6] What this and other passages like it tell us is that a Christian, biblically speaking, is one who

---

[5] Matthew 7:21–23.

[6] Jesus's answer to them as to why they are condemned is that they did not do the will of his father in heaven.

has had a radical change in their spiritual standing before God. That change should be evidenced by a changed life, but the appearance of the fruit of repentance doesn't always indicate a change in spiritual standing before God. In other words, fruit can be counterfeited. Rather than being the result of a believer's new nature, counterfeit fruit is entirely the result of an unregenerate individual's own effort. While we may have good reasons to believe that an individual has become a Christian in the biblical sense (what looks like the fruit of repentance), we can never confirm that our belief is in accordance with reality. Only the Lord knows for certain who are his.

The second meaning of the word *Christian* that's relevant to the discussion of deconversion is when a person is a Christian in a sociological sense only and lacking the ontological change in their nature that reconciles them to God. A person is a sociological Christian, as opposed to a biblical Christian, if they identify as a follower of Jesus, affirm various doctrines essential to the Christian faith, and associate with a Christian community, but remain unregenerate. In contrast to the biblical meaning of the term, which is focused on the internal and spiritual state of an individual, the sociological conception of the term *Christian* is concerned only with what is empirically verifiable. Does the individual claim to be a Christian? Check. Do they affirm basic Christian doctrines? Check. Do they attend a church? Check. Then, from a sociological perspective, they're a Christian. What the sociological definition of *Christian* does not take into account, nor could it, is whether an ontological change wrought by the Spirit has taken place in an individual's nature. The sociological lens can only see surface behaviors and attitudes. This means that it's possible that not all individuals who are Christians sociologically are Christians biblically, which suggests that it's also possible that some individuals who at one time in the past identified as Christian but now no longer do were never Christians in the biblical sense to begin with. They professed to be Christians, but they never possessed a new regenerate nature. They were merely Christians in a sociological sense, but not in a biblical sense.

The distinction between being a biblical Christian (a genuine, born-again follower of Jesus) and a sociological Christian (only demonstrating certain demographic identity markers but lacking a regenerate nature) is important to recognize in the deconversion discussion. The reason why is because, depending on your theology, you will either allow that genuine biblical Christians can deconvert, or you will be forced to conclude that deconverts, despite their protestations to the contrary, were never biblical Christians to begin with, only sociological Christians. If you fall in the former camp, then you probably see deconversion as a real problem. What could be worse than a Christian denying Christ and renouncing their faith? For you, this book addresses a real and frightening possibility. If, however, you believe that a biblical Christian cannot lose their faith, then what I am describing in this book is not a problem that the church needs to be all that concerned about. Perhaps you, like the apostle John, believe that such people "went out from us, but they did not really belong to us" (1 John 2:19). If that's the case, individuals who leave the faith are not losing salvation, they're just revealing who they really are—nonbelievers who never were believers in the first place. If you subscribe to this view, I hope you will continue reading to the end of the chapter so I can make my case for why, despite your beliefs about who can and can't commit apostasy, you should read this book.

I approach this project primarily from a sociological perspective. By that, I mean my objective is not to write a book on soteriology that argues for one side or the other of the eternal security debate. My priority is to consider individuals who believed the right things and gave evidence of the fruit of repentance at their word and, after listening carefully to their stories, try to discern what led to their loss of faith. Then, I try and see what it is that we can learn to help those we minister to and love from doing the same thing. This does not mean that the answer to the question of whether one can lose their faith is unimportant. On the contrary, it's immensely important, especially since the suggestions for discipleship or spiritual formation that I make are a result of listening to deconverts.

To make the issue plain, if an individual can't lose their salvation, then this book is not about how believers become unbelievers, but how unbelievers come to realize and reveal that they were never really believers at all. If that's the case, then any advice I offer on helping avoid deconversions would be damning. It would be so because it's based on and grounded in the testimony of those who were never really saved. To then take that information and offer advice on how we can make changes so such people will not have a crisis of faith that leads to their loss of faith (or revealing that they never had faith to begin with) is, in essence, to prolong an unbeliever's self-delusion, keeping them sociological Christians but not biblical ones. And contributing to the self-delusion that they're Christians in the biblical sense is to play a role in their eternal separation from God. Indeed, for such individuals, the loving thing to do is to allow them to deconvert. I realize that may sound harsh and unloving, but if Jesus says that knowing the truth sets one free, then if, in their experience with Christ, they were not set free, we should conclude that they never really experienced the truth. In that case, whatever it was that they were converted to was not biblical Christianity but some admixture of dead religion and biblical truth. If there is any hope of such individuals ever coming to a knowledge of the truth, they first must leave their pseudo-Christianity behind. As C. S. Lewis said, "If you have taken a wrong turning then to go forward does not get you any nearer. If you are on the wrong road progress means doing an about-turn and walking back to the right road."[7]

What Is the Gospel?

An equally important question to "What is a Christian?" is "What is the gospel?" These two questions are intimately related, and it is important that I comment on my views here as well. I have become persuaded that the word *gospel* has taken on a contemporary connotation that would have proven foreign to those of the first century and the early church. A quick Internet search for "What is the gospel?" turns up thousands of

---

[7] C. S. Lewis, *Mere Christianity* (San Francisco: HarperOne, 2015 [1952]), 28.

sites, all of which state a variation of the same theme. A good example of this theme can be found in the four spiritual laws made famous by Bill Bright and Campus Crusade for Christ:

Law 1. God loves you and created you to know Him personally.

Law 2. Man is sinful and separated from God, so we cannot know Him personally or experience His love.

Law 3. Jesus Christ is God's only provision for man's sin. Through Him alone we can know God personally and experience God's love.

Law 4. We must individually receive Jesus Christ as Savior and Lord; then we can know God personally and experience His love.[8]

While I believe the above four statements are true, I don't think they accurately reflect what the New Testament has in mind when it calls us to believe the gospel. I'm persuaded that the gospel, which simply means "good news," is a message that is larger in scope than the modern notion of the gospel presented above. In terms of the nature of the gospel, I tend to agree with scholars who maintain that the good news is not so much an offer of salvation to be received, but an announcement about a fact of reality that is to be submitted to by way of an act of fidelity. More specifically, the gospel is the proclamation that God has acted in the world to restore his rule and reign through the man, Jesus of Nazareth, by whom he will bring about the restoration of all things. It's a declaration that Jesus has appeared in order to reestablish a world of interpersonal harmony and true social justice that God originally intended for humans to experience. The means by which he has done so is by destroying the works of the devil through Jesus's death, burial, and subsequent resurrection. As a result, Jesus has established God's kingdom over which he has been exalted as the king, and he desires that everyone be part of it. That is truly good news!

---

[8] Bill Bright, "Would You Like to Know God Personally?" Campus Crusade for Christ, accessed February 5, 2020, http://www.4laws.com/laws/englishkgp/default.htm.

However, there's only one problem. As cosmic rebels, we are unfit to enter into what God is doing. Furthermore, we're not only disqualified from life with God, we are under his judgment, resulting in our eternal exclusion from what God, in Christ, is bringing about. In order to enter into the new reality that's already begun but not yet fully arrived, something needs to be done on our behalf that fixes our problem. Here is where the modern "gospel," or what I am referring to as the "message of salvation," fits into the larger, more robust gospel message preached by the apostles.[9]

Jesus's atoning sacrifice on our behalf (his sinless life, substitutionary death, and victorious resurrection) is the means by which our sin can be forgiven, we can be reconciled with God, and we can take up our unique individual roles in what God is doing in bringing about his good world. We appropriate Jesus's atoning work on the cross for ourselves by faith, defined as an attitude of repentant allegiance to him.[10] When we believe the message proclaimed about who Jesus is and what he has done, and when we appropriately respond to that message by submitting to him as the rightful Lord, we are reconciled to God and take our place as members of his family. We then look forward to the conclusion of the good news that what Jesus started he will one day finish and bring creation to a glorious consummation.

In short, the gospel proper is the good news that Jesus is the fulfillment of the story God has been telling since Genesis 3. It is the announcement that Israel's messiah and the world's rightful king has entered the world, has conquered sin and death, and is bringing to completion God's good plan for the cosmos. The message of salvation tells us how God has made it possible for us, his enemies, to enter into his good plan. He did so by the death and resurrection of Jesus on our

---

[9] Scot McKnight, *The King Jesus Gospel: The Original Good News Revisited* (Grand Rapids: Zondervan, 2011).

[10] I have become persuaded through the work of Matthew Bates, Scot McKnight, and others that when the New Testament calls individuals to "believe" in Jesus, or have "faith" in Jesus, that the connotation of the Greek word *pisteuo* is best understood as "fidelity" or "allegiance." While *trust* is also an acceptable term, *allegiance* better communicates what kind of response to Jesus that God desires.

behalf. All that's left for us to do is to respond appropriately to the proclamation about Jesus. The proper response is repentant allegiance, acknowledging that the claims of the gospel are true, and submitting to Jesus as Lord.

Can a Believer Lose Their Salvation?

When individuals who have demonstrated what seems to be a clear and prolonged Christian testimony leave the faith, it can be difficult to comprehend just how such a thing could have happened. I remember the first time I heard of a person from my circles who renounced their faith. He was the father of one of the young men in the youth group that I was leading at our church. Prior to me coming to the church to help with the youth group, Sam and his family had been missionaries overseas. Sometime after returning to the States, Sam's father had a crisis of faith that ultimately resulted in his loss of faith and the breakup of his marriage. I found out about Sam's father from one of the elders of the church. I can recall the sense of confusion that I experienced upon hearing about Sam's father. I wondered how it was possible that a missionary, of all people, could stop believing. I had no framework of understanding to process and make sense out of what I had learned. Part of the reason was that, at the time, I was unquestionably convinced of two things: one, that the doctrine of eternal security—which holds that a real Christian will inevitably make it to heaven—was true; and two, that if anyone was a real Christian, it was a person like Sam's dad, who had left everything to go and preach about Jesus among the unevangelized. It just didn't make any sense to me how a person like that could abandon his faith and his family. How could he do it?

Since this book is about people who at one time identified as Christian but who now no longer do, I think it is important to say something about the question of whether or not such people were ever saved to begin with. It seems that there are three options to choose from in answering that question. The first is to affirm that such individuals were indeed truly born-again Christians who were indwelt by the Spirit of God but no longer are, given that they have renounced their faith. The second option is to say that such individuals were never saved to begin with. Rather, they were merely professing Christians who never actually were born of the Spirit. In these cases, salvation was not lost because it was never possessed by the individuals in the first place. The third option is to see deconverts as genuine believers who are being kept by the power of God despite the fact that they profess not to believe in him. Such people will, if they are truly Christians, return again to the faith before they die.

How do I answer this question? It's complicated. On the one hand, I find it difficult, at least theologically speaking, to see how an individual who is a genuine believer can—even through their own sin and unbelief—undo the work of God in their life. I will not take the time to go into all of the theological reasons why, but it is sufficient to say that I find that the collective doctrines of predestination, election, regeneration, justification, imputation, and sanctification make the case for eternal security compelling. If salvation is a gracious gift from God that I cannot work toward obtaining prior to belief in Christ, then if I could lose my salvation by no longer believing, it would seem that I have to work hard in order to keep believing to keep my salvation. On the other hand, there are enough serious warning passages throughout the New Testament that I am left to wonder. Why, if salvation cannot be lost, does nearly every New Testament author warn believers to persevere in their belief so that they do not fall away? I've heard all of the responses from the eternal security camp and find them unpersuasive. Therefore, I am inclined to take the warning passages as referring to something that is a real possibility. Given that I have said that, theologically speaking, it seems hard to see how a true believer can become an apostate and yet, at the same time, take the warning passages directed to true believers about a real possibility of apostasy, it seems that my views on the matter are, at best, at odds with each other. Regardless, that's my position as I write. Although I wish I had more clarity on the matter, I presently have no settled position, and, to a degree, I am comfortable with that tension.

A major reason for my inability to come to a conclusion, aside from my penchant for seeing all sides of an argument, is that, ultimately, deconversion is not about doctrine—as important as it is—but about people. As with many other issues, when one knows someone who the topic under debate applies to, it can have an impact on where one comes down on the issue. Warning passages aside, I think that I would lean much more in the direction of an eternal security position if it were not for the individuals whom I have interacted with who have left the faith. It's easy to cite a few verses about salvation being eternal and claim that deconverts went out from among us because they were never of us when the people in question are nameless, faceless objects with no personality and backstory. It's another thing completely when one reads the journal of a former believer who, on page after tear-stained page, begs God to help him because he's losing his faith.

Consider a very real former believer who I'm aware of. Raised in a Christian home and committed to Christ from a young age, David wanted to be a pastor. After university, he enrolled in seminary and, upon graduating, took on a pastorate at an evangelical church in Southern California. For years, he preached sound doctrine and lead his congregation in service and worship. He was intellectually per-suaded of the truth of the gospel and had committed his life to years of faithful service. He raised his family in the faith, and he trusted Jesus in the midst of hardship. However, after years of wrestling with ques-tions he could not answer, he ended up concluding that he no longer believed that what he preached for years was true. He wept as he lost his faith, he begged God to help his unbelief, but to no avail. Today he is an unbeliever.

What are we to do with such stories? Was he never saved? I, for one, am not willing to say that. Those who believe that he wasn't saved have to provide an explanation that makes sense out of his situation. But it seems to me that all such explanations strain credulity. Inevitably, the explanation offered is that he never truly believed. Whatever such a claim means, at the very least, it means that his belief was in some way deficient. But in what way? He, as far as he could tell, believed that what he preached for years was true. Like everyone, his confidence in the claims of the Bible waxed and waned, but he was convinced enough that he committed his life to spreading the gospel message. To say he didn't have enough mental assent to the propositional claims of the Bible is hard to swallow. Maybe his belief was deficient in that it didn't translate into a life of faith? That is even harder to swallow. His life was characterized by living according to what he believed the Bible taught. Jesus was the center and circumference of his life. He had dedicated his life to full-time Christian service. What was it about his believing that was deficient?

Admittedly, most deconversion stories are not as stark as David's. And, in many cases, I am convinced that the individual who has shared with me their deconversion story or whose narrative I have read was never genuinely saved. From my limited human perspective, based on what they have said, it's obvious to me that they never really got it. It's conceivable that a large percentage of individuals who leave the faith were never saved to begin with. But in the case of some, it certainly seems they were. And given that such people exist and that, in my opinion, the biblical data is not conclusive, I am undecided whether a genuine believer can lose their faith.

Why Read This Book?

Whether a truly regenerate believer in Jesus can forfeit their salvation is an important question, but not one that this book will address. Good believers of equal theological depth and commitment have come to different conclusions on the matter. For those who believe that a genuine believer in Christ can abandon their faith, become unregenerate, and remove themselves from the body of Christ by no longer believing, the relevance of this book is obvious. If that describes you, then I don't need to convince you why reading this book is a worthy endeavor. The research and conclusions, not to mention the advice based on them, address a real problem, one that, from all accounts, seems to be growing. That is, Christians, real Christians, are leaving the faith in increasing numbers. Maybe you picked up this book in order to better understand why and how that happens, in order to discover ideas on what can be done to guard against it in the lives of those you love. For you, I don't need to offer any further rationale on why this book matters.

But what if you are reading this book and are persuaded of a more Reformed theological position, one holding that God unconditionally elects certain individuals to salvation and calls them with irresistible grace, regenerating them, and giving them the gift of faith such that a person, once regenerated and adopted into the family of God, cannot commit apostasy because they are kept from doing so by the power of God? Is there any value in reading this book for you? After all, the conclusions reached and the advice offered about how to better ground faith and avoid setting up believers for a faith crisis come from research conducted on people who, according to Reformed theology, were never saved to begin with. If that's the case, such persons haven't lost their faith—they just revealed that they never had it to begin with. And if that's true, the counsel offered below, intended to help believers avoid a faith crisis, is going to be irrelevant and maybe even counterproductive because it comes from those who were never actually believers. For those of a Reformed persuasion, it would seem that I am a bit like a researcher who is seeking a cure for emphysema, assuming that the lungs he is attempting to treat are afflicted with the disease when, in reality, they are plagued by lung cancer. Then, after finding a treatment that effectively reduced the cancer, the researcher applies it to those suffering from emphysema. But since his cure was based on the mistaken assumption that the lung cancer was emphysema, the treatment is ultimately misguided, wrongheaded, and ineffective. Likewise, so the argument goes, if true believers can't lose their salvation, then the research of this book wasn't conducted on true believers, and the advice that comes from the research is misguided, wrongheaded, and ineffective. At best, it would only help keep Christianized but unregenerate persons in the church. If a true believer can't lose their salvation, and if this is a book about "believers" losing salvation, then why read the book? What's the point? It makes as much sense as applying a treatment for lung cancer to a case of emphysema. Real Christians don't deconvert. End of story.

That's a good question and one that I believe needs an answer, especially since I believe that this book is relevant for both those who believe that genuine Christians can become apostates and for those who believe that genuine Christians cannot become apostates. My answer is two-pronged. First, assuming that a genuine believer cannot lose their salvation, it's clear to me that the issues that played a role in former Christians leaving the faith are the very same issues that cause genuine believers, those who will never leave the faith, to have some deep crises of faith that take them to the edge of apostasy, only to be kept from committing apostasy by the power of God. This is why problems raised by former believers shouldn't be ignored, even if one is convinced that they were never real believers in the first place. Clearly, there was something that brought about a crisis of faith in their life that resulted in their deconversion. Perhaps it was something that was directly related to the fact that they were never regenerated and indwelt by the Holy Spirit. In that case, it's easy to see how such a person would eventually find many of the essentials of Christianity running up against their desire for autonomy and the desires of the flesh. In such cases, not much can be gleaned from their experience that we could change in how we are communicating and passing on the faith. Doing so would compromise the very faith we are trying to pass on.

Second, after listening to dozens and reading hundreds of deconversion narratives, I am persuaded that there are a number of things not essential to the faith that did contribute to a crisis that ended in deconversion. Those are things we ought to take note of because we ought to be doing what we can to help set up believers for spiritual success without relying on the fact that no matter how badly we pass on the faith, it doesn't matter, because God will keep them saved. A parallel to what I am arguing for can be found in the proclamation of the gospel. Even if one holds a Reformed perspective on salvation, including unconditional election and irresistible grace, such a person should also believe that we have a responsibility to do everything within the bounds of faithful expediency to present the gospel in a manner that has the best chance to be understood and affirmed.

Paul, according to a Reformed reading, believed and taught unconditional election, irresistible grace, regeneration that precedes faith, and that the elect will persevere, all of which are acts of God and ensure that who God has chosen will be saved and endure to the end. Yet Paul also clearly believed that how he went about proclaiming the gospel mattered deeply in terms of people getting saved. That Paul believed how he conducted himself and how he communicated the gospel made a difference in who became a believer is not reading into the apostle's words something foreign to his thinking. Regardless of how much Paul believed in the sovereignty of God in salvation, he lived as though the salvation of the elect was dependent in some way on him. Throughout the book of Acts and his epistles, we see him doing everything in his power to communicate the gospel in ways that were faithfully expedient, contextually relevant, and without unnecessary offense in order that the gospel would receive a fair hearing.

In the First Epistle to the Corinthians, Paul finds his apostleship being questioned by certain factions in the church at Corinth. The charge against him seems to be that he is not an apostle because he does not act like one with authority. In other words, Paul does not demand from the Corinthians the financial support that should rightly be his. In response, Paul explains that he has chosen not to demand of the Corinthians that which was rightfully his for the sake of the gospel. Paul knows that if he does so, it will impede the spread of the good news. And so, he explains to them, "We put up with anything rather than hinder the gospel of Christ" (1 Cor. 9:12). He then goes on to explain how far he is willing to go in order to effectively communicate the gospel:

> Though I am free and belong to no one, I have made myself
> a slave to everyone, to win as many as possible. To the Jews I
> became like a Jew, to win the Jews. To those under the law I
> became like one under the law (though I myself am not under
> the law), so as to win those under the law. To those not having
> the law I became like one not having the law (though I am not

> free from God's law but am under Christ's law), so as to win those not having the law. To the weak I became weak, to win the weak. I have become all things to all people so that by all possible means I might save some. I do all this for the sake of the gospel, that I may share in its blessings. (1 Cor. 9:19–23)

In chapter 10, Paul encouraged the Corinthians to follow his example by sacrificing their rights for the greater good of the gospel. Instead of stumbling others by demanding the things they had a right to eat or drink, Paul commanded them:

> So whether you eat or drink or whatever you do, do it all for the glory of God. Do not cause anyone to stumble, whether Jews, Greeks or the church of God—even as I try to please everyone in every way. For I am not seeking my own good but the good of many, so that they may be saved. (1 Cor. 10:31–33)

And as committed as Paul was to the sovereignty of God in salvation, nevertheless, he wrote to Timothy: "Therefore, I endure everything for the sake of the elect, that they too may obtain the salvation that is in Christ Jesus, with eternal glory" (2 Tim. 2:10). Not that he needed to convince Timothy of the importance of removing obstacles to the gospel, for Timothy bore in his own body the evidence of his commitment to doing whatever was faithfully expedient to effectively spreading the gospel. In the book of Acts, he was willing, as a grown man, to undergo the rite of circumcision so he would not needlessly offend the Jews and place before them an obstacle to hearing the gospel. Again, Paul, as convinced as he was of the sovereignty of God in salvation, recognized that he had a responsibility to do what he could to remove barriers and present the gospel in such a way that it was compelling and attractive.

Therefore, according to a Reformed reading of Paul, God will ensure that the elect will be saved. However, as we have seen, that did not diminish Paul's sense of responsibility to do everything within the bounds of a faithful pragmatism to communicate the gospel in such a way that it was unfettered from unnecessary hindrances. I maintain that the same is true when it comes to passing on the faith, whether to our children or those in the church. In other words, how we go about discipleship matters. And, even if one is convinced, like a Reformed reader of Paul is, that God will save the elect and ensure their perseverance, one should also share in Paul's sense that he had a responsibility to work, like Paul did to ensure that the gospel message being preached was unhindered from unnecessary offenses. It is utterly consistent to believe that God will save and preserve the elect and at the same time strive to be as effective as we can be in evangelism and discipleship. If we are aware that there are practices, habits, or customs that, humanly speaking, reduce a person's ability to hear the gospel, we ought to relinquish those things. So, too, if we are aware of nonessential practices, habits, or customs that tend to hinder an individual's progress in the faith, we ought to relinquish those as well.

It may be the case that a genuine believer cannot lose their salvation. But if, and this is undoubtedly the case, the issues that former believers point to as the reason for their loss of faith are the same issues that cause faithful believers to verge on losing theirs, then listening to former believers is important regardless of whether they were genuine believers. In the next section, we will do just that: We will listen to former Christians tell us why they no longer believe, and we will discover what the process of deconversion was like. We will uncover the contexts that produced their faith exit and the strategies they utilized in navigating their loss of faith. And we will learn how losing their faith impacted their lives, both positively and negatively.

PART 2

ANATOMY LESSON

CHAPTER THREE

THE WHY OF DECONVERSION

A Leap of Faith (In Reverse)

Olympic triple jump gold medalist and BBC media personality Jonathan Edwards shocked Great Britain in 2007 when, after years of being known as a humble yet committed Christian, he came out as an atheist. The man who at one time missed an Olympic contest out of devotion to God (his event was held on a Sunday) now misses church altogether. Where once he found the existence of God obvious, he now maintains, "When you think about it rationally, it does seem incredibly improbable that there is a God."[1] Edwards, one of Great Britain's most well-known Christians, had lost his faith.

What was it that caused such a drastic change in his thinking? Edwards has not fully answered that question, but he did shed some light on it in an interview with *The Independent.* While filming a documentary on the life of the apostle Paul, he was intrigued by the suggestion from liberal scholars that Paul's Damascus Road experience was best explained as an epileptic seizure rather than an authentic religious experience. That suggestion planted the seeds of doubt in

---

[1] Matthew Syed, "'I Have Never Been Happier' Says the Man Who Won Gold but Lost God," *The Times,* June 27, 2007.

Edwards. For the first time, he began to ponder not only the question of Paul's encounter with Jesus, but all of the questions that for years he had been too preoccupied with sports to think about and had just taken for granted on the authority of the Bible:

> It was as if during my twenty-plus-year career in athletics, I had been suspended in time. I was so preoccupied with training and competing that I didn't have the time or emotional inclination to question my beliefs. Sport is simple, with a simple goal and simple lifestyle. I was quite happy in a world populated by my family and close friends, people who shared my belief system. Leaving that world to get involved with television and other projects gave me the freedom to question everything.[2]

Once the camel of doubt had snuck its nose into Edwards's tent, it wasn't long before the entire animal moved inside and took up residence. One thing that Edwards came to realize is that for all the years he was competing in athletics, his intellectual development had been in neutral. He was so focused on training and competition that he had no time to think deeply about anything else. And although he may have had a vibrant faith, it was a naive faith. The combination of being presented with an alternative reading of the Bible and the time that retirement brought created a space for him to investigate the beliefs he had always taken on faith. He eventually came to the conclusion that there simply wasn't a good reason to believe in God.

Jonathan Edwards is not alone in his loss of faith. Many people leave behind the religion of their youth. But he is unique. No two people have the same experience when it comes to deconversion. People lose their faith for all kinds of reasons, and it occurs in all kinds of ways. In this chapter, we will do two things. First, we will look at the factors that contribute to deconversion, and second, we will examine a model of the process of deconversion. In general, contributing factors, or reasons

---

[2] Syed, "I Have Never Been Happier."

for deconversion, fall under two categories: emotional reasons and cognitive reasons. Emotional reasons tend to be related to the perception of hurt by other Christians or by God himself. Cognitive reasons have to do with the truth claims of Christianity. More often than not, these have to do with problems with the Bible and the lack of evidence for the existence of God. My model of the deconversion process contains the seven stages that describe the experience of believers as they progress on their journeys from Christianity to atheism. These two aspects of losing faith are important to have knowledge of because identifying the reasons for and the process of deconverting provides a framework for understanding the impact of deconverting.

Emotional Reasons

A common complaint of former believers is that, prior to their deconversion, they were hurt by other believers, and that played a major role in their loss of faith. For some, the hurt came from being let down by the shortcomings and outright failures of church leadership. Others shared disappointments received from the hands of other Christians. For others, the impact their congregations had on them was so negative that it prompted a crisis of faith.

Disappointments with Fellow Christians

Ex-Christians are quick to point to disappointments with church leadership or those who were in positions of leadership in parachurch ministries as playing significant roles in their deconversions. I have no doubt that many former believers were hurt by other Christians. Christians can and sometimes are characterized by hypocrisy and judgmentalism. Given the fact that we are all at different places on the road to total sanctification, we should expect that our sinful tendencies will at times get the better of those of us who make up the body of Christ. Nevertheless, that does not excuse the way some former believers are treated. Deconverts are especially sensitive to the moral failing of leadership. Derek, a thirty-something male from Arkansas, said that for him it was the stealing, fraud, and sexual promiscuity running rampant among pastors he trusted that started him down the road to apostasy. No doubt any of us would find such behaviors disturbing, which would cause us to ask ourselves if what we had committed to was the truth. Instead of finding people of character in the positions of power in their churches, multiple individuals complained that the leadership they looked up to as spiritual exemplars failed miserably. Sadly, the moral failings of Christian leaders are not something that is confined to only small fringe denominations or extreme fundamentalist groups. In the past few years, high-profile, well-respected evangelical leaders have either stepped down or been removed from their positions due to serious sin. For some, it was sexual in nature; others were accused of financial mismanagement; and one was removed for emotional abuse and plagiarism. The impact on the lives of those who sat under their ministries is incalculable. Finding out that, behind the scenes, one's spiritual leaders were living immoral lives can prove too much for some to take, which is why we should not be surprised when former believers point to the failure of Christian leaders as a factor in their loss of faith.

For Charlene, a forty-year-old married mother of two in Virginia, it was not so much the moral failings of leadership that negatively impacted her faith, but how, in her eyes, the leadership in question exercised its authority. She felt that the heavy-handed approach by the elders of her church played a major role in her deconversion. In her situation, the elders refused to endorse her as a cabin leader for a preteen girls' Bible camp because, at the time, she was dating a non-Christian. Instead, they encouraged her to consider serving in another capacity, one that did not entail being an example to young, impressionable girls. While the rest of her friends were off teaching at the camp, she was required to stay home. Looking back on her experience with church leaders proved to be a major turning point for Charlene. In her church youth group, she had already proven herself to be a capable Bible teacher and leader. Nevertheless, the pastor visited her and explained that she couldn't be a camp counselor because dating a non-Christian was a bad example. Greatly offended, Charlene left the church and headed down a path from which she never returned. She surmised that since everyone already thought she was sinning by dating a non-Christian, she might as well go ahead and start genuinely sinning. She began spending more time with her boyfriend and less time with the church and the youth group. Eventually, she stopped going to church entirely.

Lauren also felt that the leadership of her church not only let her down when she most needed their help, but they completely rejected her. A thirty-eight-year-old single doctoral student, Lauren once worked at a church on the West Coast as a youth pastor and worship leader. She eventually had to leave the church to move back east to care for her ailing mother. While there, she began performing as an exotic dancer, something she did prior to her conversion to Christianity. She met a man at her club and had a child with him. They moved to Texas and lived together until he physically abused her so badly that she ended up in the hospital. After separating from him, she returned to her church community, seeking support. Shortly after returning, she met and married a man who lied to her about being a Christian in order to marry her. Devastated, Lauren subsequently began an affair with a younger man who turned out to be gay. To make matters worse, her husband refused to financially provide for her and her daughter, and they were on the brink of being thrown out of their house. Her affair and other questionable decisions became known to the pastor, and this resulted in a strained relationship between her and the church leadership. With the approval of her husband, she returned to exotic dancing in order to pay bills. When the dancing proved to be less lucrative than anticipated, her husband called the pastor to tell him of their dire situation. The church leadership informed her, through her husband, that she was, in their words, "nothing but a whore," and that if she came back around the church, they would have her arrested for child endangerment. Receiving such shocking and harsh treatment from the church leadership was the catalyst in her deconversion. Deeply hurt, her experience forever changed the way she saw her Christian leaders. They were no longer agents of God's grace but, as she described them, "horrible people." Second, she believed that the church's rejection forced her to make drastic choices in order to protect herself and her daughter from homelessness. She said the way she was treated by the leadership "actually pushed me into . . . I actually did porn for two years." In response to this experience, she wrote a column for an adult website titled, "A Family of Church vs. A Family of Porn: Which Family Really Has the Ties That Bind?" She compared her treatment within the Christian world to that of the porn industry. Looking back on her experiences with the church leadership, she said:

> I struggled for a while because I just couldn't believe that these were God's people. I couldn't believe it. . . . These are not Jesus' works. Jesus walked with the sinners. Jesus said to turn the other cheek. Jesus said, "Go out and make disciples of all nations," not "Stand on a street corner with a freaking sign, telling people they are going to hell."

Ex-Christians also spoke about how their leaders, at times, had reinforced doubts they were wrestling with. Steve approached his professor, looking for answers concerning passages in the Bible that seemed to contradict each other, and he was told that if he wanted to keep his faith, he'd be better off not asking those questions. To the twenty-eight-year-old graphic artist, the response implied that, for those in the know, there was something to hide. In his words, it was that "one statement from him that was kind of like . . . somebody saying, 'Don't go in that room; there's nothing in there. See, we keep that locked. Just walk past it.'"

It was not only Christian leaders who unwittingly inflicted hurt or discouraged former believers that played a role in deconversion, but also the perceived negative treatment that these believers received from the rank-and-file congregants. Criticism from fellow believers that he perceived as unjust or petty caused Sam, a single actor in his midfifties, to question what Christianity was all about. Because he liked to listen to pop music and watch television, he was told he was obviously a bad Christian because, if he were a Christian, he wouldn't be doing those kinds of things. Instead of challenging him to a deeper Christian commitment, it made him ask what pop music had to do with Christianity. The answer, in his mind, was that pop music has very little to do with being a Christian. This hurt was further compounded by comments that he received upon sharing with the church that he had been diagnosed with cancer. Instead of rallying around him, they told him the reason he had cancer was because he was getting a divorce. Understandably, he was offended by such reasoning and responded by pointing out that if the accusation were valid, a lot more people should have cancer because there were many bigger problems besides divorce going on in his church. Eventually, he came to the conclusion that the church had abandoned him as he went through both his divorce and battle with cancer. In return, he abandoned them.

Rachel was also going through a divorce when she was a Christian. From her perspective, when people heard that there was going to be a divorce, she started losing connection with people in her church. Although she recognized that getting a divorce while being a member of the church council created an awkward situation between her and other members of the church, the way she was treated by church members during that period led her to ask herself hard questions about her faith. The fifty-two-year-old Colorado native wondered, "What am I doing, and what is this group that I'm involved with? Do I still want to be part of it?" She concluded that the negative treatment she experienced at the hands of her fellow believers was so hurtful that she no longer wanted to be part of the church. In the end, she felt abandoned by fellow Christians, so she left the church and, ultimately, her faith.

When Martin was serving as a pastor in Las Vegas, the forty-four-year-old husband and father began questioning a few traditional positions on various social issues, and his own congregation attacked him personally and with hostility. His church was a place where questioning was looked upon negatively and doubt was pushed aside. Nevertheless, he chose to teach an adult Sunday school class in order to talk about topics such as the death penalty, LGBTQ rights, and immigration. Martin took a more liberal tack and, consequently, he found himself on the wrong end of some pointed criticism. A large number of people who showed up for the class took umbrage with Martin for his positions on the issues under discussion. After the initial class ended, Martin no longer felt welcome in the congregation, largely because of the response from the angry members who desired to get Martin and his wife fired from the staff. The church no longer wanted him to teach their children because they disagreed with him on what they felt were important doctrinal issues. His congregants' reactions disappointed and hurt him to the extent that he began to reconsider his role at the church. Shortly thereafter, he left the church. Not long after, he left the faith altogether.

Cognitive Reasons

The second major contributing factor in deconversion is cognitive challenges to the truth of Christianity and the existence of God. Every individual whom I have spoken with and all of the narratives that I have read claim that the cognitive dissonance they experienced by trying to maintain their Christian faith, in light of conflicting data, was simply too much. After wrestling with a number of different challenges to the truthfulness of Christianity and the existence of God, they no longer felt they could retain their faith with any sense of intellectual integrity. Even those whose struggle began with emotional hurts eventually left the faith over intellectual reasons. The three most significant cognitive challenges that resulted in deconversion were the following: perceived problems with the Bible, Darwinian evolution, and the influence of atheists themselves.

Problems with the Bible

For Christians, the Bible is a book without peer. It is the inspired Word of God and the final authority for life and Christian practice. Many conservative Christians affirm not only the divine inspiration of the Bible but also its inerrancy. The doctrine of inerrancy holds that the original manuscripts of the Bible were wholly without error regarding any topic they address. Furthermore, God has preserved the transmission of the Scriptures, keeping them virtually free from corruption. The Bible reveals who God is, who we are, the reason for our brokenness, and God's solution for it. This section focuses on the consequences for faith when confidence in the Bible as God's Word is lost.

Doubt about the claims of the Bible is the most common objection leveled against Christianity by former believers. Interestingly, problems raised by former believers didn't primarily come from external sources that criticized the Bible; instead, they arose from reading the Bible themselves. Christopher, an assertive and outgoing college student in Southern California, lamented, "The turning point was when I finished reading the Bible. I think it was the third time reading through it that I realized that I couldn't believe in a lot of things in it." He went on to add, "I read the Bible, and that really made me question it. The more that I read it, the more I questioned it." Wrestling with some of the content of the Bible is understandable for twenty-first-century readers. The Bible calls upon its readers to affirm a world that is often very different from their own experiences; talking snakes, angelic visitations, chariots of fire, and resurrections from the dead are conspicuously absent from their day-to-day lives. Additionally, scientists have provided explanations for many of the phenomena that the ancients would have attributed to the gods.

As one former believer pointed out regarding the veracity of the creation account, when "you have an education and you understand evolution, it is really tough to believe in a literal translation."

Reflecting on his attempt to maintain a robust faith in the Bible as an educated person, Douglas, a former Southern Baptist and now a prominent atheist activist, speaker, and author, quipped, "Boy, the mental acrobatics that we'd go through was something else!"

The doctrine of inerrancy is perhaps the cornerstone of fundamentalism and the evangelical movement. In response to the capitulation of some sectors of Christendom to the scalpel of higher criticism, fundamentalists and evangelicals strongly affirm the supernatural accounts contained in the Bible and its factual accuracy in all that it teaches. The doctrine of inerrancy, though, has not been derived from a careful empirical study of the biblical text, but is an a priori deduction from the convictions that God is perfect and that he inspired the Bible. Given these two beliefs, it logically follows that God can't inspire a text that contains errors.

As one participant put it, "When you come up fundamentalist, there are no contradictions in the Bible. It's the perfect Word of God. And if you see a contradiction, it's because you read it wrong." The problem this creates is that if one believes they have discerned a historical error or contradiction in the Bible, they must reject it as the Word of God because the sine qua non of God's Word is that it's errorless. A great deal of apologetic effort is spent in defending inerrancy by refuting biblical difficulties. Encyclopedias, books, and journal articles have been dedicated to reconciling apparent contradictions, such as the creation accounts in Genesis chapters 1 and 2 and the resurrection narratives in the Gospels. For many deconverts, the explanations, rationalizations, and harmonizations ring hollow, and they begin to doubt that the Bible is God's Word.

Interestingly, however, they do not seem to question the presupposition they have inherited from their evangelical upbringings: the belief that inspiration demands inerrancy. Like their estranged evangelical cousins, they still unquestioningly assume that inspiration demands inerrancy.

This assumption was confirmed by Douglas, who was asked, "Do you think it is generally true of deconverts that they assume inerrancy to be the case and that they have been told if there is even one error in the Bible, then it is not the Word of God?" He responded by agreeing and providing the following commentary:

> I think so. I hesitate to generalize because I've met a lot of
> people, and they all have different stories of what did it for
> them. But I think inerrancy is definitely a major part for a
> lot of people. It seems like the people who read the Bible
> the most are more likely to reach the conclusion that it has
> problems. The deconversions all hinged on a different part,
> but, sooner or later, they reach their tipping point. Definitely
> for me, the Bible having errors was definitely a factor. I was
> taught to guard the truth and defend the truth. Then I find
> out these Christian beliefs are all lies. When you find out that

this thing they call the truth may not be *the* truth—boom!—
that did a number on me.

Douglas was not the only person I spoke with whose beliefs were shaken by a perceived contradiction in the Bible. Steve was also powerfully impacted by his discovery of what he claimed he knew to be a contradiction in the Bible. He estimated that, while growing up, he had read the Bible twenty times, cover to cover, but while at a Christian liberal arts college, he came across what he referred to as "the contradiction." As he read through the Bible, he encountered what he was convinced was an irresolvable problem, and he was floored. He decided to turn a critical eye back to the Bible and began to reread. He took three months and went through it again, and by the time he had finished, he estimated that he had forty pages of notebook paper filled with contradictions and difficulties.

The Bible is a record of many events that seem morally suspicious, if not offensive, to contemporary readers. The problem for some deconverts is not the record of morally offensive events, like the slaughter of the Canaanites, but that God ordered the atrocities. If one has inherited a particular view of God, one that focuses only on his kindness and love, then when one encounters such troubling stories, this can cause a sense of disequilibrium. How could the good and loving God of the Bible command such heinous acts, like slaughtering all of the inhabitants of the promised land?

Martin had such an experience when he encountered the stories of what he took to be genocide in the Old Testament. The dissonance was so great between his view of God and what the Old Testament recorded that he expressed that he felt lied to about the Bible. He elaborated by pointing out the many troubling stories of divinely sanctioned violence in the Bible, specifically what he referred to as stories of genocide. It was also difficult for him to reconcile the God of the Old Testament, whom he saw as angry and violent, and the God of the New Testament, whom he saw as loving and gracious.

For Anne, the problem related less to the moral problems with the God of the Bible and more with the historicity of the text. While attending a Christian college, the thirty-five-year-old Las Vegas resident was required to take courses covering both the Old Testament and New Testament. The first course looked at the New Testament and exposed her to issues she had apparently never considered, such as the process of canonization and textual criticism. The course caused her to question the trustworthiness of the New Testament. Hearing about the books that did not make it into the New Testament, the process of canonization, the variations between manuscripts, and the questions about authorship caused her great distress. She began to question the reliability of the New Testament as a historical document and whether there were enough good reasons to trust it as the foundation for her life. The second-semester course on the Old Testament added to her doubts. However, this time it wasn't issues of canonization and textual criticism that were the problems. What caused her to question the trustworthiness of the Old Testament was the combination of apparent contradictions in the exodus account and the absence of extrabiblical evidence for the exodus itself:

> The second semester, I took Old Testament. It was actually the story of the exodus; we were reading it. The accounts, they seemed completely contradictory. There were things about it . . . just things that were not logical that really bugged me. I couldn't understand the Egyptians not recording the exodus in their history, especially if two-thirds of their labor force just up and left. That would have a huge economic impact on their society, and for it to never be noted, I thought that was strange.

The result was a series of confrontations with her professor and pastor in which she expressed her anger at never having been taught that information before. The cumulative effect on her faith was substantial. The classes had planted seeds of doubt that would grow into unbelief:

I remember marching into my professor's office and becoming really belligerent and crazy, angry that nobody had ever taught me about the Apocrypha or the history of the Bible. I had a lot of heated conversations with my pastor back home about it. It was really tough because it was, like, my first exposure to "Maybe this isn't valid?"

Darwinian Evolution

A commonly mentioned factor in deconversion is the acceptance of Darwinian evolution as the explanation for the origin of all species. Multiple deconverts mentioned that accepting the theory of evolution played a role in their deconversion. For deconverts, the belief that the entire edifice of organic life could have evolved through random, beneficial mutations over time struck a major blow to their theistic worldviews. While many believers, when presented with the evidence for Darwinian evolution, manage to retain their faith by becoming theistic evolutionists, the deconverts in this study appear to have presupposed that, for various reasons, if evolution were true, then God could not exist. Convinced of the truthfulness of evolution, they believed they were forced to reject belief in God's existence.

In response to the question "Can you point to anything specific that you would identify as a catalyst for your loss of faith?," a quarter responded with comments such as "Learning about evolution is a powerful thing for me"; "Understanding the theory of evolution is like the biggest thing for me"; and "Evidence of evolution was one of the biggest things." Many deconverts raised in Christian homes were only taught the creationist account of origins. Evolution was not a legitimate theory of origins in the experience of many former believers, since holding to both the theory of evolution and Christianity would produce cognitive dissonance.

The fact that most deconverts were raised with the traditional creationist account of origins meant that often their first exposures to the theory of evolution were in high school or, for some, even as late as college. Marcus, a soft-spoken student at UCLA, noted, "I don't think

I'd ever really explored . . . a secular worldview before I was fifteen. Once I started taking biology and opening myself up to those ideas a bit more, that was kind of like my first exposure to that. It turns out I agree with that more."

The timing of the exposure to the theory of Darwinian evolution is not insignificant as it relates to deconversion. During late adolescence and early adulthood, people begin to think critically about their worldviews. The influence that teachers and professors have on students at this point in life can be significant. The combination of assuming science to be the final authority for truth claims and meeting evangelistic Darwinians can be a potent source for doubt. In the case of Marcus, he was taking a biology class at high school taught by an engaging and knowledgeable student teacher from a state university. The teacher frequently brought up the conflict between theism and atheism and creationism and evolutionism. He was not shy about his atheism and about how evolution scientifically accounted for the origin of species, whereas creationism was based on blind faith that contradicted science. Marcus credited the influence of the knowledgeable and affable teacher as the first step toward leaving his faith.

For Douglas, striving to keep belief in creationism when, in his heart of hearts, he knew evolution was the "real deal," was difficult for him. Likewise, Mitch wrestled with how to process the evidence for evolution and what it meant for his faith. Mitch, a nursing student who wanted to serve in emergency rooms, had a crisis of faith. After being convinced that the evidence for evolution was persuasive, he realized his new position on origins would impact the contour of his faith. It was clear to him that one couldn't be an evolutionist and a Christian. Unlike others, he did explore the possibility of adopting a theistic evolutionary viewpoint, but he found that it created more problems than it solved:

> When I read through the evidence on evolution, I wondered at what point was the soul imparted? Did God come down and touch a prehuman hominid with a soul? Was it Australopithecus? Do they have a soul? So that question

was one that, as I started struggling with it, had a big impact on me.

Accepting Darwinian evolution proved to be a cognitive challenge to the faith of former believers. Most claimed that belief in God and belief in evolution were incompatible. When they became convinced that the evidence pointed toward evolution, they were left with two choices: follow the evidence and accept evolution as their theory of origins, or ignore the evidence and sacrifice their intellectual integrity. For the former believers, following the evolutionary evidence entailed denying the existence of God. One former believer attempted to reconcile evolution and theism but believed that it could not be done without producing significant cognitive dissonance.

The Influence of Atheists

The New Atheists are a cadre of authors from different backgrounds who are united in their disbelief in the existence of God and in their conviction that religion is a force for evil that should be abandoned for the good of all. Their scathing critiques of arguments for the existence of God and withering criticisms of religion have earned them a wide hearing in a post–9/11 world. The most influential of the New Atheists are sometimes known as the Four Horsemen: Richard Dawkins, Daniel Dennett, Christopher Hitchens, and Sam Harris.

Dale, a lawyer practicing in the greater Los Angeles area, read Richard Dawkins's book *The God Delusion* and encountered an unfamiliar argument for why God probably does not exist. He found it persuasive and realized that, if true, he could no longer be a believer. He picked that book because he had been involved in informal debates about the existence of God. Dale was convinced there was enough good evidence to believe in God, but he wanted to hear the other side's arguments. As he read, he realized he accepted one of the arguments made in the book. Despite his best efforts, he was unable to refute the argument and felt compelled to acknowledge that it was unlikely that God existed. He was clear as to why he lost his faith. "It wasn't a decision that I made because I was unhappy with my belief or a conflict that I had seen in the church. It wasn't because of any social and personal conflict. It was just the logical argument that I accepted."

Mitch also attributed his loss of faith to reading the works of the New Atheists. Ironically, he did so while serving as a full-time employee at a Bible summer camp. He and some Christian friends in a small group began slowly exploring, from a very guarded perspective, the atheist worldview. He was wary because, as he put it, "It's a pretty brutal attack straight on your faith, bringing a lot of questions." Despite the brutality of the attacks, he continued to devour their books. He particularly enjoyed the writings of Sam Harris and, over time, resonated with Harris's withering criticism of theism, Christianity, and religion in general. Eventually, he concluded that Harris and the other atheist authors he read were correct: There is no God, Christianity is false, and religion is dangerous.

Apologetic material is ubiquitous for Christians. For decades, Christian publishing houses have been churning out apologetic books, and Christian radio stations have aired apologetic preaching, defending and arguing for the faith. Entire ministries are dedicated to the task of apologetics, and some of evangelicalism's most prominent representatives are apologists. Atheism, however, lacks the infrastructure that is inherent in a religion like Christianity. For instance, there are few atheist bookstores and publishing houses and even fewer atheist radio stations in the United States. Seekers cannot drive across town to the local atheist bookstore to pick a book on atheist apologetics. In fact, it was nearly impossible for the average person to access atheist apologetics until recently. Consequently, millions of Christians have been exposed to only one side of the argument for Christianity, and that may create an unchallenged sense of confidence that reason and evidence demonstrate the truth of Christianity. With the advent of the Internet, all that has changed. In many ways, the Internet is the great equalizer in the world of ideas, and for atheism, it has proven to be the ideal platform for challenging the claims of Christianity. A quarter of participants credited the Internet for providing them with information that contributed to their deconversions.

Mitch offered the following observations about the importance and influence of the Internet on deconversion:

> I think Dan Dennett is the one [who] thinks the Internet will completely change the future. I feel . . . that the Internet has opened and raised my consciousness to a point that I have very different priorities on what's important, as opposed to what I did before I had this information. The Internet started opening my eyes that the atheist movement had been out there.

Initially, he was just curious. He recalled looking at websites and reading stories about people losing their faith, but he was convinced that that would never happen to him. He was aware that studying atheism might change his perspective to some degree and give himself a greater sense of sympathy for atheism, but he did not think he would change his mind. And yet, after spending copious amounts of time reading discussions on the atheism thread at the Reddit website, he did just that.

Douglas has also seen how the Internet can cause believers to lose their faith. However, in his case, it's not the influence that the Internet had on his deconversion, but the influence he is having on the deconversion of others via the Internet. Douglas is an active online atheist evangelist. Thanks to the Internet, his message has reached a vast audience around the world. He claims that he receives emails from people in Egypt and elsewhere in the Middle East and from women who have lost their Christian faith because of his website. He attributes the reason why he receives so many emails from women to the fact that in the Middle East, women are often discouraged from working or driving. They tend to stay at home and, with little else to do, go on the Internet. Douglas pointed out that in their countries, anti-Islamic websites are banned, but there are plenty of anti-Christian websites they can access, including his.

Wayne, a computer technician from East Texas, once identified as an amateur apologist. He too identified the Internet as a major influence in his deconversion. He was in college when the Internet became widely available. He spent time online for the purpose of meeting new people. In doing so, he realized that most of the people he met online were not Christians. This fact made him question the truthfulness of Christianity, since it meant that the majority of the people he knew would spend eternity in hell. To resolve this issue, he watched debates of noted Christian apologist William Lane Craig on YouTube. Trying his best to avoid confirmation bias, he thought through both sides of the argument. In describing his strategy, he said, "If I could consider the arguments that the atheists have and refute them to my satisfaction, then I'm good. I don't have anything to worry about." Unfortunately, he couldn't refute the atheist position. He began to notice that the more videos he watched, the more inclined toward atheism he became.

The Process

No doubt there are many more reasons why deconverts lose their faith than the categories I listed above. Every person is different. For some, it's an acute crisis brought on by a particular doubt or bad experience. For others, they're afflicted with what Phil Zuckerman calls "acquired incredulity syndrome" (AIS).[3] AIS is Zuckerman's term for the inability to continue to believe in the face of growing contrary evidence. Eventually, those with AIS leave the faith because they can no longer make themselves believe in a worldview that, over time, has, in their mind, been demonstrated to be false.

Knowing the reasons offered by individuals who lose their faith is only part of the picture. Equally important is the question of how they lose their faith. What does the process look like? What are the steps? Is there a point of no return once a person begins the process that leads to deconversion? We will tackle these questions and more in the next chapter.

---

[3] Phil Zuckerman, *Faith No More: Why People Reject Religion* (Oxford: Oxford University Press, 2015).

CHAPTER FOUR

THE HOW OF DECONVERSION

Trusting the Process

In 1969, Elizabeth Kübler-Ross published a book titled *On Death and Dying*, based on her research on terminally ill patients. What the Swiss American psychologist purported to discover was that individuals facing a diagnosis of terminal illness progress through five stages of grief. The first response is denial. Here, individuals are unwilling to accept the diagnosis, preferring to believe that a mistake has been made and that, despite the evidence to the contrary, they have been misdiagnosed. Stage two is characterized by anger. When it becomes impossible to deny the fact of the matter, individuals accept the diagnosis but become angry at what has happened to them. Sometimes the anger is directed toward those who are closest to them. For those who believe in God, it is typical to direct anger at him for allowing the individual to become sick. Bargaining, or hoping that the individual can avoid death, is the third stage. Individuals in this stage often will promise God that they will change their lifestyle if only he will heal them. Bargaining tacitly acknowledges that the individual is aware of aspects of their life that are inconsistent with the will of God and could be the reason why they have become ill. Depression marks the fourth stage. Coming to terms with the fact that their proposed bargain is not going to deliver them from their fate, individuals can become despondent. Common behaviors that characterize this stage include refusing visitors and expressing depressive thoughts. The final stage of the process is that of acceptance. In the last stage, individuals accept their mortality and that the future has been written. Ironically, in the final stage, when one might expect an individual to grow more despondent, the recognition that death will soon take their life is met with a calm, reflective view and relatively stable emotions.[1]

Since its publication, Kübler-Ross's work has come under scrutiny. Not everyone agrees that the stages she identified have enough empirical support to justify them as five unique stages. Others have noted that clinical observation does not always support the existence of the five stages. For example, the five stages are not always experienced in a neat linear fashion. Kübler-Ross herself has said that the stages do not have to be linear, nor do all terminally ill individuals have to experience all of them. What nearly everyone does agree on, however, is that when dealing with tragic, life-altering news, individuals go through a process of grief in order to cope. There are few things in life that are not characterized by a process; from falling in love to baking cakes, our lives are characterized by events that comprise stages. Some are rigidly lawlike and do not allow for skipping stages. Others are less austere in their progression but are, nonetheless, procedures that have identifiable phases.

A particularly good example of a process that, while not rigidly lawlike, does have commonly identifiable stages, is the process of religious conversion. Few individuals commit to a new faith without first moving through several phases that take them from being an unbeliever to a believer. There are examples of sudden conversion—the apostle Paul, for one—but the overwhelming majority of religious conversions come as the result of a process. The authoritative work on religious conversion is *Understanding Religious Conversion* by Lewis Rambo. His study shed light on a century's worth of research on conversion. Rambo

---

[1] Elizabeth Kübler-Ross, *On Death and Dying* (New York: Scribner Classics, 1997 [1969]).

argues that all conversions go through the same process but than none are ever identical. Every conversion is unique in the specific details, but Rambo maintains that there are six stages to all conversions: context, crisis, quest, encounter, commitment, and consequences. All religious conversions arise out of a particular context. Context, for Rambo, is both a macro- and micro- concept. The macro comprises the cultural, sociopolitical, economic, and ecological factors that may either assist or frustrate conversion. The micro is made up of the immediate aspects of an individual's life, including his friends, family, religion, and even neighborhood.[2] Like the macro-context, the factors that make up the micro-context can also facilitate or obstruct conversion.

The second stage in the process, crisis, is an experience that's characterized by a sense of disorientation. This crisis may be religious, political, psychological, or cultural in origin.[3] Crisis can either be events that cause an individual to question their fundamental orientation to life or something milder, but which acts as the straw that breaks the camel's back.[4] The third stage in Rambo's model, quest, is where the individual begins to seek a resolution to the sense of disequilibrium that has resulted from the crisis event. This is an intentional act on the part of the future convert and is something they do, as opposed to something that happens to them.

Fourth, the quest to resolve the crisis often leads an individual to what Rambo calls an encounter with a member of a different religion. Such a person may be a religious colleague who they know, or a religious professional such as a pastor, guru, or missionary. Encountering a person of faith who one finds credible and winsome can lead to the fifth stage of conversion, interaction. This stage involves intentional investigation and engagement with the new religious perspective. It may include attending religious services, reading literature, and learning to pray. The focus at this stage is on what it means to be a new spiritual

---

[2] Lewis Rambo, *Understanding Religious Conversion* (New Haven: Yale University Press, 1995), 22.

[3] Rambo, *Understanding Religious Conversion*, 44.

[4] Rambo, *Understanding Religious Conversion*, 46.

being.[5] Stage five can last for an indeterminant length of time, but at some point, the individual will either move on to the sixth stage or will terminate the process because they've concluded that the claims of the religion in question are either not true or at least not something they are willing to commit themselves to. If, after a period of interaction, an individual decides that the religion they're investigating does provide them with the answers they're seeking, they'll commit themselves to it, which is the sixth stage in the process. At this point, the individual may participate in a ritual that acknowledges their conversion to the new faith. The rituals perform the action of creating a new identity, set of relationships, and set of roles that lead to a new kind of life.[6] The seventh and final stage of Rambo's conversion process model is the consequence phase. In this phase, the individual experiences the result of their decision to convert. The changes that take place can be intellectual, emotional, spiritual, and so on, and if the changes are perceived as being good and beneficial, then, in all likelihood, the conversion will take, and the individual will remain a lifelong believer.

Theologian Scot McKnight has argued that "theoretically speaking, all conversions are apostasies and all apostasies are therefore conversions."[7] If that's true, then Rambo's model of the process of conversion should be helpful in understanding the process of deconversion. In his work *Finding Faith, Losing Faith*, McKnight argues that each stage of Rambo's model is detectable in the vast majority of deconversion testimonies. I tend to agree with McKnight, and my own research is largely consistent with Rambo's model.

The model presented below is based on information provided by former Christians who I interviewed, as well as published deconversion accounts. The model that emerged consisted of seven stages: (1) context, (2) a crisis of faith, (3) seeking to know the truth, (4) trying to retain

---

[5] Lewis Rambo, "Lewis Rambo Extended Interview," *Religion & Ethics Newsweekly*, PBS, November 10, 2000.

[6] Rambo, *Understanding Religious Conversion*, 124.

[7] Scot McKnight and Hauna Ondrey, *Finding Faith, Losing Faith: Stories of Conversion and Apostasy* (Waco: Baylor University Press, 2008), 7.

the faith, (5) moving to agnosticism, (6) becoming an atheist, and (7) coming out as an atheist. My research shows that when it comes to those who once self-identified as Christian, a surprisingly large number find relief as they move toward atheism.

Like myself, researcher Julie Krueger has identified similar stages in the deconversion process.[8] Three of those stages correspond with three stages of the model presented here. Her deconverts also experienced a stage of doubt, migration away from the faith, and finally, apostasy. Where our studies differ is that Krueger's don't begin with crisis but with weak social attachment. Deconverts' weak social attachment led to doubt about the truthfulness of Christianity. From that point, deconverts disassociated from their faith communities and transitioned away from their Christian identities. In the final stage, they declared their identities as atheists.

A third model that is worth noting is one developed by John Barbour in his highly respected work, *Versions of Deconversion: Autobiography and the Loss of Faith*.[9] Barbour's approach to uncovering the deconversion process is to analyze the autobiographies of notable religious deconverts, including Augustine, John Henry Newman, Edmund Gosse, Jean Paul Sartre, and John Ruskin. Not all of the deconversions were away from Christianity. Augustine, for example, was a deconvert from Manicheanism to Christianity. Regardless of which religion they deconverted from, Barbour notes several commonalities in the autobiographies. The first is intellectual doubt or denial in regard to the truth of a system of beliefs. The second is moral criticism, which entails rejecting the entire way of life of a religious group. The third is the experience of emotional suffering, including grief, guilt, loneliness, and despair. The fourth and final commonality is disaffiliation from the religious community.

---

[8] Julie Krueger, "The Road to Disbelief: A Study of the Atheist De-Conversion Process" (master's thesis, University of Wisconsin–La Crosse, 2013).

[9] Jonathan Barbour, *Versions of Deconversion: Autobiography and the Loss of Faith* (Charlottesville: University of Virginia Press, 1994).

Of particular note is Barbour's second category focusing on moral criticism. Former believers, according to Barbour's analysis, move from losing belief in the truth claims of a religion to then finding moral fault with it. While neither Rambo, Krueger, nor I identify this as a stage in the deconversion process, nevertheless, in many, if not the majority of, deconversion narratives, moral criticism of Christianity is a prominent feature. Perhaps this is due to the fact that individuals who share deconversion stories online or subject themselves to interviews do so because they want to express their criticism of Christianity. Maybe those who do not have an axe to grind about Christianity do not tend to publish their deconversion testimonies. Regardless, Barbour's observation that an aspect of moral criticism is common among deconversion narratives is important to take note of because of what it may tell us about the kind of Christianity they rejected. I have come to the conclusion that after listening to the stories of former believers, the version of Christianity they rejected was worthy of much of the moral criticism they leveled at it.

The Deconversion Process

The following is the model of deconversion that emerged from the interviews and narratives that I analyzed. As previously mentioned, it consists of seven stages that move from Christian commitment to the consequences of identifying as an atheist. Not every person matriculated through each of the seven stages. However, each of the seven stages featured prominently in the majority of the cases.

Stage 1: Context

Deconverts emerge from all walks of life. Some are professionals; others are blue-collar workers. Many are college-educated, but some are not. They arise from rural and urban locales, and they can be any age, but more than likely they are between eighteen and thirty years old. And yet, with all the contextual differences that frame deconversion narratives, one dominant feature stands out. A disproportionate number of deconversions have in common a similar type of Christian background.

Repeatedly, deconversion stories exhibit aspects of fundamentalism. We will look closer at just what that means in Chapter Five. For now, it is enough to note that while some former Christians testify that their home and church experiences were gracious, loving, and life-giving, the vast majority do not. On the contrary, more often than not, they have little good to say about their time as Christians. Words such as *strict*, *narrow-minded*, *legalistic*, and *fundamentalist* are commonly ascribed to their Christian experience.

Stage 2: Crisis

The deconversion process begins with a crisis of faith. A significant event occurred that caused the believer to question his or her faith. Each crisis was unique to the individual, but every person reported a crisis moment. Three broad classifications of crises emerged from the stories of the individuals: bad experiences with other Christians, exposure to virtuous non-Christians, and confronting intellectual challenges to the faith.

Steve recounted an experience with his mother when he revealed to her that he had decided to make contact with his estranged father and his father's new wife. Steve's mother told him that he only had one mother in God's eyes, so he had to choose his father's new wife or his mother. Steve refused to choose, and he let her know he wasn't going to play her games. The result is that, tragically, she has not spoken to Steve or his sister in eight years. The rationale Steve's mother used to justify her extreme choice to cut her two children out of her life is based on her understanding of what the Bible teaches about marriage. Steve saw this action as one in a long list of tragedies engendered by religious irrationality. He credited experiences like the one with his mother for making him more receptive to what he would read from the New Atheists. He said,

> Christopher Hitchens, in his *God Is Not Great*, provides an alphabetical list of different kinds of atrocities in basic religious teachings and showing good and bad getting flipped. I was thinking, "I can really attest to that firsthand."

Sam's crisis came through the treatment he received from other Christians in his church. He saw the church as more of a social club with rules, and if you didn't follow these rules, you wouldn't fit in. By questioning what he perceived as the legalism in the church, he believed he became less popular with his own group of Christian friends and within his congregation. The crisis reached a peak when he started divorce proceedings. To him, it was clear how much outside of the social club he was at that point, so he decided to step back, reevaluate, and think about what he really believed in terms of his faith.

Interacting with others who were not Christians but were good, moral people challenged the particularist presuppositions of some former believers. Their uncritical acceptances of the exclusive claims of Christianity were difficult to retain in the faces of their experiences. Donald provided an excellent example. A former member of the military who served in Iraq, he struggled with the thought that a Muslim he had come to know and admire was consigned to hell because he was of a different faith. He recalled having specific and meaningful conversations with a Muslim man who had been assigned to his platoon in Iraq. The man was born and raised in Iraq and had gone through many tragic experiences under Saddam Hussein. He served alongside US forces as a regiment translator, trying to help the Americans rebuild the country. As a translator, the Muslim man used to go with Donald and his unit to assist them in interacting with the population. They worked together on a daily basis for a year in order to achieve the goal of creating a better Iraq. As a result, Donald got to know him quite well. Spending as much time together as they did led Donald to become curious about the Muslim faith. A dialogue ensued, and Donald found himself learning what it meant to be a Muslim. The outcome of this interreligious dialogue was that it caused Donald to rethink some of his previously held beliefs. Specifically, he started thinking that, according to his parents and his church, his Muslim friend and fellow soldier was condemned to hell. Naturally, he struggled greatly with the idea of someone like his friend going to hell because he was a Muslim. He lamented:

I had the hardest time reconciling that. Here was this guy, he was married and had children, [and] he was trying to do what he thought was best for his family. For me, he was a good, moral, decent person, and just because he has a different faith, he is going to hell. That, I just couldn't accept. That sort of started making me question Christianity.

The third crisis point was general intellectual doubts about the truth of Christianity. Although problems with the Bible were the most specific objections raised by former believers, all, at some point, raised general intellectual problems with Christianity. For some, it proved to initiate the deconversion process. In the case of Sam, along with how he was treated by his church friends, his doubts were strengthened when he read an atheist book intended to disprove Christianity. It dawned on him that he had no honest argument in response. He concluded that everything that was said about Christianity for the last thirty years was, for him, now under scrutiny. More problematic was the thought that he didn't have a single comeback to the arguments in the atheist book.

Dave is a self-identified humanist activist. Combative and confident, he raised the perennial intellectual challenge to the existence of God, the problem of evil: How can it be reasonably said that God is loving, in light of the gross amount of evil in the world? His statement powerfully captured the problem and is worth quoting in full:

> When we look at the problems in the world, when we look at starvation, tornadoes, hurricanes, leukemia striking children, earthquakes crumbling [structures] down and trapping people under these giant blocks (obviously, they can't move), these terrific events in our lives are terrifying, and when we insert a God into the equation, that adds thousands more questions. Why would it say in Psalms 121:7, "God is going to keep us from harm," when clearly that's not the case? Atheists and Christians experience harm at the exact the same statistical rate. Why, if people are in fact biologically born gay, would they also be immediately condemned to a life of never

experiencing love, or in Leviticus 20:13, be killed because of their actions in simply acting out of love? Why would a God of love condemn someone for feeling love when he's the one that made it that way, when, in fact, he made them that way? Why doesn't God lift the rocks in Haiti? Why doesn't God cure the children from leukemia? It creates this cognitive dissonance that God is love, and yet he watches as these horrific things happen, and he does nothing to stop it. I would stop it if I could, and I'm just an atheist.

Plagued by questions, Charlene couldn't help but wonder why her non-Christian friends gossiped less and were more genuinely generous than her Christian friends. When she raised the issue, she was reminded that everyone is human and that it was not up to her to judge anyone. To make matters worse, she was told that she thought too much and was too smart for her own good. Far from satisfying her curiosity, that response led only to more questions, specifically about the relationship between God's sovereignty and human responsibility. She asked, "Didn't God make me this way? Wasn't he the one who gave me my intelligence and the ability to ask questions?" If so, she wondered, why was she to blame for her inquisitiveness?

Stage 3: Seeking the Truth

At the second stage of the deconversion process, believers began to seek ways to resolve their crises. Not content to merely ignore the challenges and continue with the status quo, they choose to seek the truth. As Christopher put it as he struggled with his doubts, "I really wanted to know what the real truth was." Some, like Wayne, first looked to God for help. For about a year, he suppressed his doubts, afraid to take steps to resolve them. Over time, a sense of apathy set in regarding his faith. Occasionally, he prayed, asking God to help him with his doubts and asking for reassurance or direction where he could look to find resources that would bolster his faith. Eventually, he branched out in the opposite direction and started looking at top atheist resources on the Internet in order to learn about how atheists think and what they believe. He began his search by walking into his office, sitting at his computer, going to Google, and typing "Atheist." The rest, as they say, is history.

Dave, upon experiencing a crisis moment during his baptism, realized that he had never really investigated whether what he believed was true. As he stood in front of the entire church in the baptismal tank, he had a crisis moment. The weight of that moment made him realize that he needed to put in more time and effort to figure out whether what he was about to commit himself to was true. After the baptism, he literally ran home, grabbed a bottle of water, and sat down with his Bible and read it for hours. He managed to get through Genesis and Exodus before he was overwhelmed with questions. This crisis that began when he was fifteen lasted into his early twenties. He sought out theology professors, biblical scholars, and philosophers in hopes of answering his growing list of questions because, as he put it, the truthfulness of Christianity "was the single most important question of my life. It was my eternity that was at stake." That acute onset of doubt generated in Dave a passion for finding the truth. His study continued to raise even more questions for him about what he believed. He continued researching and, as he did, it became more difficult to hold onto his faith. It is at this point, in the face of counterarguments and objections, that believers make the move to the third stage.

Stage 4: Trying to Retain Faith

The third stage of the deconversion process involves believers attempting to retain their faith in the face of growing doubts. It was at this stage when several individuals in this study turned the corner in their journeys to atheism. A majority skipped this step altogether, capitulating quickly when challenged either emotionally or intellectually. Those who resisted reported that, despite their desires, they could not maintain belief in God.

Charlene spoke about her "path from Christian to atheist as a conversion experience." For her, "It took years of painful, sometimes excruciating, struggle" as she "slowly awakened into reason."

Wayne, likewise, went through a lengthy period of wrestling with what he believed. Shortly after becoming a father, he "started having some pretty serious doubts." Until then, there wasn't a point when he didn't believe. When doubt came, his strategy for dealing with it was ignoring it. He managed to avoid doubt for quite some time, but it eventually caught up with him. "It was actually in my thirties, the first time I actually seriously thought that I maybe I don't believe this anymore," he said. Dale also wrestled with holding onto his faith in the face of increasing doubts:

> I wouldn't describe it as ever having chosen atheism. I tried
> very hard in the two months following to convince myself back.
> I read a lot of Francis Collins. I've read a lot of Lee Strobel,
> reread a lot of previous arguments in favor of God, trying to
> convince myself that God really exists because I thought: (a) It's
> a big deal. I should not make this move lightly. And (b) it was
> a way I could save my marriage, so I tried very hard for social
> and personal reasons to hold on to Christianity.

The impact of attending a Christian college and being exposed to ideas that challenged a rigid interpretation of the Bible forced Mitch to find a way to hold on to the core of his faith and accept the new ideas he was learning. His strategy was to "liberalize a little bit" in his positions. He believed that he "started to question things, trying to reconcile the existence of an eternal hell with the existence of an all-loving, all-powerful God." He found himself also "trying to reconcile issues about science" and the Bible "in order to maintain a belief in God" in light of the new data he was encountering.

Stage 5: Going from Believer to Agnostic

At the point in the process where retaining belief in God was no longer feasible, some chose to identify as agnostics before they became atheists. Slightly more than half of the former believers I spoke with at one time were agnostics; the other half transitioned from being believers to atheists without an intervening step, or they did not use the term *agnostic*.

Martin, who worked in a pastoral role at church as an agnostic, said, "By the time I was at church . . . you know, working at an office in the church, I came to terms with the fact that I was actually agnostic. I didn't believe anymore. I think it was more about working in the church and having the paycheck."

Steve abandoned his belief in the Christian God but did not immediately become an atheist. He still believed there was a supernatural essence to reality. He speculated, "Maybe something bigger is out there, but maybe it's like energy, or the cosmic consciousness, whatever the buzzword of the year is." The uncertainty of what ultimate reality was caused him to linger in epistemic limbo for more than two years before he moved from agnosticism to atheism. Shelley, a middle-aged resident of the Pacific Northwest, also spent two years as a full-blown agnostic as she sought the truth. In the end, Martin, Steve, and Shelley, like all the others in the study, matriculated to stage six and identified as atheists.

Stage 6: Going from Agnostic to Atheist

Moving from agnosticism to atheism marked the penultimate stage of the deconversion process. All former believers who shared their stories with me and identified as agnostics at one time eventually migrated to atheism, although it must be noted that the definition of atheism adopted by the vast majority of those I spoke with is functionally no different from agnosticism. Traditionally, atheism has been understood to affirm the nonexistence of God. Recently, however, many atheists have chosen to define their position in the negative, such as "lacking a belief in God." Christopher is a good example of the conflation in terms:

> So, I became agnostic first, and it's only because I started having doubts. It was one thing to figure out how do you clear up those doubts. It wasn't until later on that I considered myself an atheist. Like now, I consider myself an agnostic atheist, which means I don't make an assertion that there is no God—that is the agnostic part—but I'm also unconvinced, so that's the atheist part.

What all of the participants seem not to realize, however, is that it is difficult to distinguish the lack of a belief in God from agnosticism. Moreover, it does not rise to the level of being a genuine philosophical position because it makes no claim about reality. Instead, it merely reports an individual's subjective, inner mental state.

Stage 7: Coming Out as an Unbeliever

Once an individual admits to themselves that they no longer identify as a Christian and that they are an agnostic or an atheist, they are faced with a choice of telling others about their loss of faith. Coming out as an unbeliever can be very costly. For many deconverts, leaving the Christian faith is much more than rejecting a set of beliefs. Because of the role belief structures play in constructing the world and situating us within it, they provide us with a sense of identity and security. But despite how hard it can be to lose one's belief system, deconverts testify that it's the loss of relationships that is the greater loss. Christianity is much more than a set of beliefs—to be a Christian is not only to give mental assent to certain essential doctrines, but to also be part of a community of believers. Often, that community comprises family members and other individuals with whom deconverts have become close with. For some individuals, it isn't uncommon that the church and its members encompass all of their social relationships. When that's the case, losing faith can sever most, if not all, of an individual's friendships, leaving them feeling alone and alienated. As we'll see in Chapters Six and Seven, along with the loss of a worldview and a community, there are numerous other negative consequences experienced by coming-out unbelievers. And yet, at the same time, despite all of the negative consequences, deconverts consistently report that coming out was worth it because of the positive consequences they experienced. We will look at what those experiences are in Chapter Nine.

The Point of No Return

It is virtually impossible to identify a point of no return in deconversion narratives. By "point of no return," I mean that place in the deconversion journey where if an individual goes beyond, they will not return to the faith. The reason for that is because there are numerous examples of individuals who have gone all the way to the end of the process and renounced their faith, only to subsequently return to faith at a later point. I am familiar with several Christians who walked away but returned and today identify as followers of Jesus. Having said that, however, I am of the opinion that after listening to and reading deconversion narratives, a point of no return can be identified, if only tentatively so. Yet this point isn't found primarily at a particular stage in the process, but in the attitude of the individual going through the process. When believers begin to harbor or express anger and moral criticism toward their faith, they have reached a dangerous place in the deconversion process. What anger reveals is that a believer has encountered a challenge to their faith that has convinced them not only that it is untrue, but that they have been deceived by the church or their parents into living a lie. Some of the most hostile former Christians were at one time those who were deeply committed to Christianity.

As a result, they were willing to sacrifice things they enjoyed, like sex, secular music, movies, alcohol, and so on, in order to be faithful Christians. Or they participated in activities such as evangelism, mission trips, and attending Bible college, even though it caused them to be seen in an unflattering light by their non-Christian friends and family. Encountering an intellectual objection that is particularly powerful, experiencing a deep wound from other Christians, or thinking that God isn't meeting their expectations are all key factors in the deconversion process. But each one of these can be overcome if an individual is willing. Like a good marriage counselor, a wise pastor or a fellow Christian can help struggling believers to maintain a relationship with God, as long as there is the will to do so. But if individuals feel deceived or betrayed to such an extent that their anger prohibits them from engaging in a therapeutic dialogue intended to overcome the feelings of hurt and betrayal and restore a sense of trust in God, then apostasy is an almost inevitable result.

The End of the Process

How people lose their faith is a challenging question. Deconversion is a complex life event that resists being easily explained. And yet, at the same time, the testimonies of former Christians display a discernable pattern. The model of the deconversion process that emerged from my research reflects many of the same features that Lewis Rambo's model of conversion identifies, as well as that of Julie Krueger's deconversion model. My model is constituted by seven stages: (1) context, (2) crisis, (3) truth seeking, (4) trying to retain the faith, (5) moving toward agnosticism, (6) moving from agnosticism to atheism, and finally, (7) coming out as an atheist.

While being able to say something about how people lose their faith is important, a more thorough understanding of deconversion is required, and other contributing factors need to be identified. One of the most significant factors playing a role in faith loss is the context from which a person deconverts. All of us live within communities that provide us with both ethical and epistemological norms and which shape our identities. Communities may be founded on family ties, ethnic heritage, political beliefs, social interests, or religious beliefs, to name but a few. Such communities are instrumental in shaping us into the persons we're becoming. They also give us a sense of belonging and meet our need for interpersonal relationships. Communities have great influence over us, and being aware of them can help us understand ourselves better. Similarly, identifying and understanding the contexts from which deconverts emerge can help us better understand the phenomenon of deconversion. Therefore, the question is, what kind of environments tend to produce deconverts? It is to that question we now turn.

CHAPTER FIVE

CONTEXT IS EVERYTHING

I'll Never Be Your Beast of Burden

A number of years ago, the host of a popular Christian television show and his wife were engaged in a lively discussion with their guest, a man who claimed, "My ministry is based entirely on my life verse, Matthew 19:26, '. . . with God all things are possible.' God gave me that verse because I was born in 1926."

Fascinated, the host of the show began looking through the Bible for his life verse. "I was born in 1934. My life verse must be Matthew 19:34—what does it say?" Unfortunately, he discovered that Matthew 19 has only 30 verses.

Undeterred, the host continued on to the book of Luke, found chapter 19, and read verse 34, which says, "And they said, The Lord hath need of him" (KJV).

Excited, he exclaimed, "Oh that's the verse! The Lord has need of me!" Thrilled, the host had finally discovered his life verse. That was until his wife pointed out that the verse is making reference to a jackass.[1]

---

[1] John MacArthur Jr., *Charismatic Chaos* (Grand Rapids: Zondervan Academic, 1993), 102.

All good exegetes know that the number one rule of interpretation is that in order to correctly understand a passage, one must first determine the context. In order to do that, one has to take into account the historical and literary setting of the passage in question. To ignore the context of a passage of Scripture runs the risk of arriving at interpretations that are not only wrong but, as the talk show host discovered, embarrassing. The same is true when trying to gain insights about events. The circumstances surrounding events such as deconversions are important to consider because they are the soil out of which the loss of faith grew. If we want to understand the loss of faith better, we need to understand the contexts such losses are commonly associated with. We ignore taking context into consideration at our own peril because, in doing so, we are likely to draw wrong conclusions about why people leave the faith.

The previous chapters looked at the reasons given by deconverts for why they lost their faith, offering a model of the process of deconversion. Two main factors contributing to deconversion were identified: cognitive and emotional. Each of the factors was subdivided into further sections and expanded upon. This chapter focuses on the contexts out of which deconversion emerges. The background conditions in which deconversion occurs have a significant bearing on the impacts. For example, the fact that former believers report overwhelmingly positive results from deconversion speaks to the nature of how they perceived their Christian experiences. Testimonies revealed that, for the deconverts, the factors surrounding their deconversions made abandoning their faith feel like liberation from an oppressive system. Three aspects that make up the context from which the narratives emerged were: (a) aspects of fundamentalism, (b) high Christian commitment, and (c) problems with Christianity while being a Christian. Not every former believer cited the above factors, nor did any one participant report all of them. However, the four themes were prominent in the narratives of deconversion, and they provide an important glimpse into the contexts within which deconversion occurs.

Fundamentally Problematic

While fundamentalism is difficult to define, there are certain attitudes and behaviors that typically characterize it. Fundamentalism is often associated with an approach to religious faith that emphasizes the avoidance of taboos, an embrace of anti-intellectualism, a demand for keeping unspotted from "the world," a narrow-minded and religious exclusivism, and a negative posture to those outside the faith. Other attributes that are identified with fundamentalism, such as legalism, wooden literalism, and an overly strict commitment to a particular church, are frequently present in the narratives of former believers. It is not surprising that many deconverts reported being reared in environments that they perceived as being fundamentalist. The focus on what not to do and who not to associate with left them with a bad taste in their mouths and acted as precursors for their deconversions. Few spoke fondly of their religious upbringings.

Thou Shalt Not

A hallmark of fundamentalism is an emphasis on taboos: prohibited actions, items, and beliefs. The rationale behind taboos is certainly justifiable from a biblical perspective. There are ample texts in Scripture that tell believers what they are not to do. And being a follower of Jesus does require believers to set him apart as Lord and resist conforming to the world. The problem, however, is not the existence of taboos, but when the focus becomes almost exclusively on what Christians are not to do. When that happens, Christianity becomes a religion of works, but not works that are meritorious in nature. Instead, great effort is exerted on avoiding sin and conformity to the world. Loving God and enjoying him forever take a backseat. Naturally, in order to avoid sin, one needs to know what sin is, and Christian communities that place a high value on avoiding sin never seem to be in doubt as to what sin is. Tragically, more often than not, the list of taboos that different fundamentalist communities maintain are based more on the tradition of the community than Scripture. To compound the problem, such communities are typically characterized by an all-or-nothing, black-and-white approach to living the Christian life, where keeping the rules is the end goal. Martin was raised in such an environment. He described the religious environment in which he was nurtured as strict. He shared, "My parents are pretty strict, I mean, we were a pretty strict religious family. By that, I mean we never missed a church service; there was Wednesday night and Sunday morning up to evening." He went on to elaborate just how strict his parents were. Not only did they never miss a church service, they also had very narrow beliefs about who was and was not Christian. While it is unclear if others outside of his denomination were considered believers, it is clear that those who were Roman Catholic were not: "You know, I was raised that I shouldn't associate with Catholics—that's how strict the household that I grew up in was. And, Catholics really weren't Christian you know; they prayed to Mary and other stuff."

He emphasized the importance of avoiding all the things that Christians shouldn't do. In his home, vices like alcohol were not only frowned upon but were viewed as a horrible thing for a Christian to do. Eventually, for various reasons and over the course of several years, Martin lost his faith. No longer a Christian, he was free to rethink his beliefs concerning just about every area of life. As one might expect, as an adult atheist, he no longer believes that drinking is evil. So, when he dines out with his parents, he, to their chagrin, often orders a beer. Ironically, even though the greater issue is the fact that he no longer identifies as a Christian, his parents' concern lies not with that but with the fact that he drinks alcohol. When he orders an alcoholic beverage, they get upset and tell him he shouldn't drink because it's sinful. Rather than trying to restore him back to the faith by loving him well and engaging him in respectful dialogue, they are fixated on managing his behavior, which is on their list of taboos.

Growing up as a member of a minority sect, Tim, a fifty-three-year-old drummer in a rock band, described his home life in rural North Dakota as strict and staunchly religious. He attributed much of that to his father who, perhaps unwittingly, was lured by the power and control that the fundamentalist church gave him over his family. Tim alleged that his father was the one who was most enthusiastic about

Christianity because Christianity, according to Tim, gives fathers all of the power in the home. From Tim's point of view, everything in his home revolved around the church in his formative years. This meant that Tim missed out on many of the things that others his age got to participate in. Naturally, this produced in him a feeling of resentment toward Christianity. The rigidity of his father's version of Christianity acted like a straitjacket for him. Instead of providing him with an abundant life promised by Jesus, it deprived him of even the average joys that his friends experienced as they attended dances, played sports, and went to movies. The emphasis by parents and church leaders to protect their children from the harmful and dangerous aspects of the world seems for many deconverts to have backfired. Rather than keeping their young people from the corruption they saw in the world, they drove them to it by making the many things that for them comprised "the world" all the more alluring.

Derek also described his religious upbringing as strict and fundamentalist. In his experience, it wasn't so much the taboos and restrictions that negatively impacted his view of Christianity, but more the rigid and wooden literalism that was demanded in reading the Bible. Regarding how one should interpret the Bible, Derek was told, "Take it literally or not at all." Being presented with a take-it-or-leave-it approach to the Bible was instrumental in his deconversion. As he explained, "When I found things I couldn't take literally, I just pulled on the string, and it kind of unraveled." Derek's story is a classic example of what has been referred to by some as a house-of-cards faith. A house-of-cards faith describes a belief system that's inflexible, fragile, and always in danger of collapse due to the nature of its construction. By its very nature, every card in a house of cards is necessary for the tower to stand. Pull out just one card, and the entire structure collapses. It doesn't matter what card it is—pull it out and down goes the house. Just as a house of cards will fall if one card is pulled out, so too does the all-or-nothing belief system assumed by former Christians. Like Derek, former believers frequently reveal that theirs was an all-or-nothing faith. The reasoning underwriting this kind of faith is driven by four key assumptions. First, it's assumed that "real" Christians believe and submit to everything the Bible teaches. There's no picking and choosing. Jesus is Lord of all or not at all.

Second, it is assumed that unless one is a "real" Christian, then they are not Christian at all. Many may profess to be followers of Jesus, but the proof is in the pudding. Only those who are sold out to Christ are really Christians. Third, fundamentalists assume that what they have been taught simply is what the Bible teaches. They are largely unaware that what they have been taught is a take, or an interpretation, of what the Bible teaches. In other words, they assume that what they believe is just the unadorned, unfiltered, pristine teaching of Scripture.

Fourth, they assume that if the Bible has an error, it cannot be the Word of God. Unsurprisingly, when they become convinced of a claim that's at odds with their literal interpretation of the Bible, they're left with no other conclusion than the Bible is errant. And if the Bible is errant, it cannot be the Word of God. There are variations on the house-of-cards type of faith. Not every former believer who shows evidence of a house-of-cards faith believes that the Bible needs to always be interpreted literally. But almost all former believers whose faith resembled a house of cards assumed that their interpretation was simply just what the Bible taught. There is a glaring lack of exposure to the various other ways Christians have interpreted the Bible throughout church history. Many deconverts assume that their uniquely American, evangelical, fundamentalist, early-twenty-first-century version of Christianity is identical with biblical Christianity. When they become disillusioned with their idiosyncratic version and reject it, they conclude that it's biblical Christianity they are abandoning, when in reality, what they have rejected many times is only a poor expression of it.

Steve's home was a good example of the kind of environment that is characteristic of other aspects of fundamentalism, legalism, and hypocrisy. In his home, keeping the rules his parents believed the Bible prescribed was of utmost importance. In order to be a good Christian, he was expected to live according to a long list of dos and don'ts. Besides the fact that the list was overbearing and burdensome to keep, the bigger problem for Steve was that his parents didn't live according to the same standard they held him to. The most damning comment about the dangers of an overly restrictive religious home life came from Shelley. She believed her upbringing was not only strict but abusive:

> Well, I do look at what I went through as a form of child abuse. What they did to me was abuse, and it did affect my life in negative ways. I didn't feel that my parents were intentionally abusive because they followed what they thought was good, but what I did experience was mental abuse. And, it had a negative impact on me throughout my childhood and my high school years. And, my college years—they were very, very difficult for me. I wished I didn't have to go through that.

Anti-Intellectual

At some point in life, most people find themselves wondering about what are sometimes called the big questions of existence, such as: What is the meaning of life? Who am I? Does God exist? If so, how can I know? Which religion is true? Questions like these are natural and display a level of emotional and psychological maturity that is healthy. They are signs that an individual is transitioning from the uncritical acceptance of ideas that is characteristic of childhood to becoming an intellectually responsible adult. As parents and church leaders, we should be encouraged by such questions, especially if we believe that the Christian faith has good answers to such questions, unless we're afraid that such questions demonstrate a lack of belief and are a harbinger of apostasy. Ex-Christians commonly speak of being reared in environments that are plagued by that very fear. Therefore, their church communities discouraged the asking of challenging questions and critical thinking. From listening to former believers tell their stories about their interactions with church leaders and parents, three reasons emerged why asking questions was discouraged.

First was the inability of parents and church leaders to answer questions. As a way of avoiding the embarrassment of not having answers, they discouraged deconverts from asking questions they couldn't answer. This is somewhat understandable; no one wants to feel foolish about being unable to answer questions about something as important as one's faith. Second, answering questions is challenging. Asking questions is a lot easier than answering them. No one needs to be an expert in order to raise questions, but providing good answers often requires putting in time and effort. Furthermore, the Internet has exposed thousands of believers to doubts and forms of skepticism that otherwise would have never occurred to them. But providing quality answers to such a wide array of challenges can be very hard. Whether the questions pertain to science, historical criticism, or philosophy, giving intelligent responses requires training. But well-trained individuals are few and far between. It's not hard to imagine an average parent who loves Jesus but is not a trained apologist choosing to discourage the asking of hard questions in lieu of answering them, due to their inability to do so.

Third, voiced questions have a way of forcing the one who is being questioned to face uncomfortable challenges to their faith, which they themselves have suppressed. Feeling threatened by questions and the danger they pose to one's faith, the strategy adopted is to discourage questions out of fear for what might be found if answers are sought.

Fourth, and most important, questioning one's beliefs is discouraged because it's interpreted as a lack of faith. The assumption here is that believing is something that doesn't need to be warranted—and, in fact, shouldn't be. Real belief, according to this way of thinking, is characterized by a kind of irrational leap in the dark. Seeking answers to difficult questions is seen, against this backdrop, as lacking in faith. Therefore, critical analysis, investigating the claims of the Bible, or wanting to find answers to doubts is seen as antithetical to faith. Indeed, by finding answers to questions, one's faith is diminished since having faith means not having reasons for what one believes. That being the case, if faith is the premium virtue that one needs in order to be a Christian, asking questions and seeking answers to ground one's faith ought to be discouraged.

Regardless of the reasoning behind the suppression of critical inquiry, such suppression is an important contextual factor in the deconversion process. Charlene's home was characterized by unquestioned devotion to a way of life, the effects of which lingered long after her deconversion. Her childhood was so marked by unquestioning devotion to Christianity, the belief in a supernatural being, and commitment to God's will that asking questions felt to her like an act of betrayal. Shelley was also discouraged from asking questions and perceived the leadership as requiring blind obedience:

> When I was a Christian, it had to be a certain way because I was told it had to be, or that's what my church told me, my pastor or the deacons. . . . I had to be a specific way. I was taught not to question my elders, especially not to question the people who were part of my spiritual life.

Cindy, too, was not allowed to ask questions concerning her faith, which ultimately resulted in her inability to be assertive and think for herself. Sadly, it caused the forty-two-year-old from Simi Valley, California, to place her trust in people who didn't have her best interest at heart, leading to undesirable consequences: "I was taught to never question anything, so that's why I was so naive and passive growing up because I didn't question anything and that made me trust people whom I shouldn't have trusted."

Negative and Critical

Although they were meaningfully committed to their faith and seeking to become like Jesus, deconverts generally viewed themselves as critical, negative, and judgmental people. They spoke regretfully about the attitudes they had toward those outside the faith. Rather than loving their neighbors, they admit that they looked down on them. This will become evident in Chapter Nine, when the discussion moves to the perceived benefits of abandoning the Christian faith, but for now, only one example is necessary.

Rachel looked back on her time as a Christian with embarrassment and anger because she felt it made her disrespectful of other people who didn't hold the same beliefs as her. She reserved her greatest disdain for those who believed in evolution, which she believed was a convenient excuse to avoid being responsible to God. Her belief in creationism was directly tied to her judgmental attitude:

> If anybody would say they were an evolutionist, even if they had a PhD in biology, I discounted pretty much everything they said. I wouldn't even listen to them. I think I was probably rude toward individuals, not respecting the people and work they had done and the knowledge they had gained because I would discount it right away. And, I think now the fact that I didn't have any degree for one thing, I didn't have any knowledge in that way is now a humbling thought. I would think, "Because I have the Bible, I have this righteousness that I'm right, and you're wrong, and I don't care how much study you have done. Clearly, you don't believe in God, so you kind of don't know what you are talking about."

Rachel is far from being alone when it comes to feeling regret for her attitude toward unbelievers. Other former believers share her sense of embarrassment at how they treated others. They frequently ascribe attitudes of superiority and arrogance to themselves when they were Christians and to their former Christian communities. Believing that they were on God's side meant that they had all the answers and that it was easy to look down on those who disagreed with them. For Rachel and others, not only were such people wrong in their beliefs, but their errors were due to their hardness of heart. The error of their ways could be traced to their unwillingness to believe (Rom. 1:18–32; Eph. 4:17–19). They were the kind of people the apostle Paul described as those who professed themselves to be wise but, in reality, were fools (Rom. 1:22). Therefore, looking down on and criticizing non-Christians was warranted, regardless of what the issue was.

High Christian Commitment

Contrary to what one may assume about individuals who leave the faith, it is common for deconverts to exhibit an above-average commitment to the faith or their church prior to exiting. During their times as believers, church attendance was a regular occurrence for those who shared their stories. All but two former believers I spoke with reported that the church played a significant role in their lives. Some attended because they were still under the authority of their parents, but others went willingly, of their own accord. Not all deconverts were raised in the church, but those who were tended to be raised in families that placed a high priority on going to church and had a commitment to being there whenever there was a service. For some, the commitments of their families to church caused them to suffer in various ways.

Despite the fact that there were a number of Christian churches in their hometown, Martin's family chose to drive an hour and a half, round trip, twice on Sundays, to their particular church:

> We actually drove almost forty minutes to the church one-way.
> I grew up south of Dallas in a really small town. The town had
> Baptist and a lot of other Protestant churches, but my parents
> chose to drive almost forty minutes away to Dallas. That's
> how my parents were. Only when we got older, my sister and
> I started complaining about sitting in the car for almost two
> hours, round trip, twice a day on Sunday.

Douglas's family also was deeply committed to church attendance. Their commitments extended beyond church to a home group that met at his house and also extended to participation in the youth group. Nearly every day of the week had a church-related activity. Sunday morning, Sunday evening, and Wednesday night were regular all-church meetings. Thursday night was a home group at his house. Tuesday night was a home group at someone else's house. Friday night was youth group. Douglas found his family's commitment to church attendance overwhelming. But what really turned him off was that it prohibited him from doing things that other kids his age were doing outside of school.

Sports, hanging out with non-church friends, and other non-church activities were made impossible due to his family's high commitment to the church.

Not only did former believers come from families of high commitment to Christianity, but prior to their deconversions, former believers themselves exhibited behaviors characteristic of committed Christians. Twenty-two of the twenty-four individuals demonstrated high levels of commitment to their faiths. It is clear from the data that all the participants considered themselves Christians and were serious about their faith prior to deconverting. For some, that meant teaching Sunday school; for others, it meant going to seminary. The interviews revealed a willingness to serve, worship, pray, study the Bible, engage in dialogue with others, give money, and deny certain proscribed pleasures. The amount of biblical knowledge varied from person to person, and their understandings of what it meant to be a Christian was by no means uniform. However, each person deconverted from, what was in his or her mind, a context of meaningful Christian commitment.

For example, looking at Steve's life when he identified as a believer reveals someone who seemed to be completely sold out to Christ. Desiring to serve, share the gospel, and worship God, he showed a zeal not often seen among Christian youth:

> I was in any church opportunities that were available. I did
> summer stuff like King's Kids, where you go to a camp and
> you learn god-awful choreography in pastel shirts and go and
> perform it on the street and stuff. I went with a group called
> Teen Mania; it does international missions. I went over to
> Russia with them and to Ireland and Jamaica with my church
> youth group. I would say that I was about as into it as you
> could be. You know Acquire the Fire, Ron Luce's big thing?
> I would go and rededicate myself, and I was, yeah, I was on
> fire. I was on the worship team at the private school when
> I went to a Christian college. I was on their Thursday night

band kind of thing and did mission trips with them. I was in it
about as hard-core as you can be into it.

Charlene appeared to be deeply committed, and she possessed a passionate desire to follow Jesus. Her life produced what, at the very least,
looked like genuine, spiritual fruit. She rededicated her life to the Lord
at a weekend retreat, and she threw herself wholeheartedly into Bible
study, youth group, and mission trips. She even won a friend or two
over to Christ at her high school. These converts joined the youth
group, then the church, and today still identify as Christians. Jill, a
city worker in San Francisco in her midforties, also regularly attended
Sunday school as a child and later taught Sunday school as well as a
high school church class. She even spent time at a Bible camp where
she worked for a number of summers.

What all of the above examples demonstrate is that nearly all former
believers considered themselves genuine, authentic followers of Jesus
at one time. In their mind, there is no doubt that they truly believed
and were committed to the faith. This is why they bristle at the most
common answer Christians give for the loss of faith, which is that they
never really were believers in the first place. This same frustration is
repeatedly expressed by ex-Christians online and in many autobiographies in print. Nothing is as insulting to former believers as explaining
away their apostasy by asserting that they never truly were believers. If
I have heard the following claim once, I have heard it dozens of times:
"If I wasn't a real believer, then no one is a real believer."

While the purpose of this book is not to address the doctrine of
eternal security, I would like to make at least one comment about it that
I believe is relevant to the topic at hand. After interviewing dozens of
former believers and reading hundreds of deconversion narratives, I
have come to the conclusion that, many times, the claim by Christians
that former believers were never saved is nothing more than a convenient way of avoiding the complexity of the situation. I suspect that it
also arises less as a result of sound theological reflection than it does
out of the need for security. If a true believer can lose their faith and

commit apostasy, then it stands to reason that the person leveling the accusation may also do so. The thought that there is a real possibility of losing one's faith can be threatening and is avoided by merely denying the possibility. I am not suggesting that a regenerate believer can commit apostasy. I am only suggesting that the knee-jerk response that such former believers were never saved is not helpful, even if true.

Not with the Program

Prior to their deconversions, 75 percent of former believers identified with a theological position, social issue, or lifestyle choice considered aberrant by their conservative Christian communities. In some ways, despite their high level of commitment, former believers did not fit in ideologically before they deconverted. What is interesting about this contextual category is that it raises the obvious question of whether some deconversions were more a matter of not liking Christianity and wanting it to be untrue more than finding it untrue and deconverting. Of course, there is no way to know, and a charitable interpretation requires that they be taken at their word. At the same time, there is good biblical reason for suspecting that deconversion is as much a matter of the heart as it is the head. Willful suppression of the truth (Rom. 1:18), being willingly ignorant (2 Pet. 3:5), and having minds that are darkened due to the hardness of their heart (Eph. 4:18) are all characteristics of our broken humanity. Moreover, despite deconvert protestations to the contrary, Jeremiah 17:9 still stands: "The heart is deceitful above all things and beyond cure. Who can understand it?" The reports of former believers and how either their experiences or beliefs did not line up with Christian theology leaves the question of their salvation a genuine one.

Unsurprisingly, there were theological issues that bothered deconverts when they were still believers. What they were told about God, as opposed to their own moral intuitions, acted as precursors to their deconversions. The primary theological issue involved was the supposed goodness of God, specifically the doctrines of God's sovereignty in salvation and eternal punishment. Frank, while a theology student at a college in Pennsylvania, struggled with God's sovereignty from the beginning of his college career until he deconverted. "I had struggled from day one in Grove City with the problem of God's sovereignty. Calvinist interpretations of that troubled me. How can God create people just to condemn them? That made God evil." He tried to reconcile this inconsistency in his beliefs by adopting a fideistic approach to his faith that allowed him to avoid seeking a rational answer to the question. However, that strategy was ultimately unsuccessful because it did not override his moral sensibilities. He had already come to the conclusion that the God of the Bible was an immoral character, and, despite his attempt to retreat into fideism as a means of reconciling moral tensions, he could not manage to do so.

Martin wrestled with the doctrine of hell. He complained about the injustice of God condemning a good man to hell just because he believed the wrong things. The apparent unfairness of being consigned to eternal punishment because of holding the wrong beliefs caused Martin to question his entire belief system for the first time. He recalled, "That sort of started making me ask questions about things like Christianity. Why would God punish a [good] guy?"

Tim also struggled to understand the rationale behind the doctrine of hell. For the musician and atheist activist from North Dakota, it seemed ridiculous that any God worthy of the title would send people to hell over insignificant matters like the ones that were important to his church:

> There were things our church said were sinful such as men with long hair or women with short hair. Those are the things that the church was completely hung up on. I was like, "What has that to do with anything? Okay, he has long hair, she's got a pixie haircut, does that affect other people? Are we going to hell because of a haircut? That would be really stupid. What kind of petty, petty deity would believe that?"

It wasn't just doctrinal issues that gave deconverts pause; it was also the positions their churches took on social issues. Within evangelical Christian circles, there has traditionally been broad agreement on social issues that the Bible regards as sinful. Included in that list is the practice of homosexuality. And yet a third of the individuals I spoke with testified that, while Christians, they did not share the majority view that homosexuality is wrong. For them, the moral position regarding homosexuality was that the church was wrong in condemning it.

Sam had been involved in the performing arts for years and, subsequently, had come to accept homosexuality as a legitimate expression of sexuality. In his daily life, he had many friends who were gay. Because he witnessed their lives and the love they had for him and each other, he found it difficult to agree with the church he attended that their lifestyle was sinful. His advocacy on behalf of gay marriage put him further out of step with the church. Tim shared the same perspective as Sam. He, too, had come to the conclusion that homosexuality is not a sin before he deconverted, which made it difficult to justify being a member of a faith that did.

One former believer with views on homosexuality that were outside the bounds of his church tried to get the church to see things his way. While a member of his church, Martin actively worked to change the minds of people in his congregation about homosexuality. He and a small group of like-minded friends worked to get the church to change its bylaws and accept active gay and lesbian people as members. He also worked for change within the denomination by advocating for the rights of gay and lesbian congregants at the church's general conference.

It is impossible to know if the theological conflicts, lifestyle choices, or contrarian positions on social issues held by deconverts were convenient excuses to reject a faith they no longer wanted to follow. That is certainly one option. Another option is that participants found Christianity in such tension with their own reason, moral sensibilities, and desires that they were motivated to look into the truth claims of Christianity and subsequently became convinced that it was untrue. Whatever the case may be, the problems they had with Christianity were important background conditions that related to the impacts of their deconversions.

What Else Do You Expect?

The combination of the reasons identified in the previous chapter and the background conditions highlighted in this one begin to paint a picture of why deconversion happens. Explaining what causes deconversion is complex and can't be reduced to a simple equation. The best we can say is that certain reasons and contexts are highly correlated with the loss of faith, but we can never say exactly what causes it. What can be said, with confidence, is that what I discovered in my conversations with former believers is consistent with what repeatedly appears in online and print deconversion narratives, which is that fundamentalist church environments are breeding grounds for deconverts. Of the five contextual factors influencing and shaping the experiences of participants, aspects of fundamentalism appeared most often. The rigid, legalistic, overly conservative beliefs and practices that parents and church leaders were convinced represented true Christianity for former Christians was a burden that proved too heavy to bear. In the end, like the Christian Pilgrim in *Pilgrim's Progress*, they only experienced relief when they let it go.

Laying down the burden of their faith produced numerous and significant positive impacts for deconverts. We will address those shortly. But before we do, it is important to take a hard look at the negative impact of losing one's faith and leaving one's community. Because serious religious faith affects every aspect of one's life, when faith is renounced, it impacts identity, relationships, values, beliefs, and innumerable other areas. For those who were committed to their faith, both in terms of belief and lifestyle—such as the individuals who shared their stories with me—the loss of faith often has devastating consequences. In the next chapter, we will spend time considering what some of those are.

CHAPTER SIX

SUFFERING THE CONSEQUENCES

Counting the Cost

The American War of Independence lasted from 1775 to 1783. When the war ended, the colonies had secured their freedom from Great Britain and became the United States of America. Being free from the monarchial tyranny of King George III produced great benefits, including a constitution and a Bill of Rights that over time resulted in the abolition of slavery in 1865. But the cost of freedom was high. The war killed thousands of colonists, created conflict within families between those who supported the war and those loyal to the Crown, and required borrowing millions of dollars from France and the Netherlands, putting the Americans into massive debt. It is to be expected that an event as momentous as a country winning its independence is bound to come with significant negative consequences. Changes at such deep and profound levels have a ripple effect across every aspect of the country.

Something similar also occurs when individuals renounce their religious faith. Going from being a committed believer and member of a church community to being a nonbeliever, devoid of a faith community, comes with significant negative consequences. In both cases, the War of Independence and the deconversion from an oppressive religious faith, freedom has been won but at great cost.

Unquestionably, there are numerous negative consequences to deconverting from Christianity. Renouncing one's worldview often comes at a high premium. Christianity acted as the lens through which each of the individuals who spoke with me interpreted the world. It answered questions such as the following: What is the nature of ultimate reality? What is a human being? How do we determine right and wrong? What happens after we die? Where is history going? It also was the context within which nearly all of the individuals had been raised, and it was the social world in which they operated. Thus, it provided both the foundation upon which their worldviews were built and the social contexts in which they developed. Upon renouncing their Christian faith, they experienced significant negative social, emotional, occupational, and existential consequences.

Negative Social Impact

The single greatest negative impact of deconversion was felt most acutely in the loss of relationships. Former believers consistently report that the negative impact that resulted from deconverting was overwhelming. Three specific areas in which the impact was most intensely experienced was in relationships with family, close friends, and even the community at large.

Parents

Of all the family relationships that experienced negative consequences resulting from deconversion, perhaps the relationship where the impact was felt deepest was with parents. Parents, as a unit, were referred to by participants as expressing a range of emotions, from disappointment to denial. For some parents, it was harder than others to hear the news. What differentiated each case was how deeply committed to Christianity the parents were. Those who were more committed were more upset than those who demonstrated less commitment to the faith.

Coming out as non-Christian to his parents was not easy for Douglas. Regardless, he felt that he needed to tell them the truth. So, he sat them down and told them he was no longer a Christian and that he identified as an atheist. Accepting his atheism was not easy for them. Both were shocked, and, as Douglas described it, "It just blew their minds"—especially his mother, who, he fondly recalled, freaked out. His father did not respond in the way Douglas thought he would but was nonetheless not happy with his son's decision. His relationship with them became strained, and things have not improved with time. His lifestyle and activities continue to drive a wedge between him and his parents. The most difficult thing for him was coming home for Christmas and being asked what he had been up to that year. He shocked everyone by telling them that he had been writing erotica and leading an atheist study group that searched the Bible for errors when he wasn't traveling the country speaking about how Jesus never existed! Needless to say, that only increased the ever-widening gap between him and his parents. The rest of the evening was spent answering a slew of questions that only made Douglas feel more alienated from his parents than he previously did. Unsurprisingly, for a long time, his relationship with his parents was awkward and strained. Eventually, they reconnected, but it was only after they found enough common ground on which to rebuild their relationship. Nevertheless, Douglas said the strain on his relationship with his parents was the toughest aspect of his faith exit.

Going home and being around his parents for lengthy periods of time was difficult for Mitch as well since they no longer shared the same faith. Like Douglas, finding things to talk about with his parents was difficult. For Kristen and her husband's parents, the problem was not that they did not have enough in common to talk about since their deconversions, but that his parents insisted on talking about it so much that the married mother of two and her husband had to erect boundaries to curtail the discussions:

> My husband's parents are the ones who have the biggest problem with our deconversion. But we have eventually come to a point where we set up boundaries that limit how much we discuss religion. If they continue to respect those

boundaries—which took years to make happen—then things will be okay. If not, we will have less contact with them.

Mothers

It is clear that the parent who suffers the most from a child's deconversion is the mother. For whatever reason, ex-Christians' relationships with their mothers have suffered more than any other family relationship. The relationship between faithful mothers and unbelieving children was often greatly strained, and a mother was more likely to attempt to reconvert the deconvert than any other family member. Charlene and her mother often argued over Christianity as Charlene was losing her faith. She described the experience for her mother as heartbreaking. As a result, Charlene used to hide her convictions from her. Now she lives her life as openly and honestly as she can without pushing her beliefs on her mother. They no longer fight because they don't talk about religion anymore, which is far better than no longer fighting simply because they no longer speak at all.

The most moving story of the hurt experienced by both a participant and that participant's mother came from Jill. In recounting one of her last visits to see her mother in the hospital, she was moved to tears as she said:

> I was there at the hospice her last few days, and she wouldn't acknowledge me. She told my sister that she thought I was going to hell, so she turned her face away from me, and she didn't ever speak to me. She talked to others, but she never spoke to me.

Jill's mother passed away without ever speaking to her daughter again. When Dave revealed to his mother that he was no longer a Christian, she assumed that he was just going through a phase. She refused to believe that he no longer believed in the existence of God. When he first told his mother, she didn't believe him, and instead believed that it was just something he was going through, something he would come out of with his faith intact. She told him that he was just angry at God because of what he thought God had done to him. She indicated that she was confident that he would nevertheless return to God. Dave described her as being in complete denial and, over time, his unbelief only strengthened to the point that he is now a committed atheist. One reason it got worse was that she perceived him as trying to convert her to atheism. Once Dave became aware of that and changed his approach, their relationship improved. He realized that it was his approach that was the source of much of the problem. This motivated him to reframe how he talked to his mother about issues of faith. He could see that she perceived him as trying to convert her to atheism just as a Mormon or Jehovah's Witness missionary might try to convert her to their religion. To clear the air, he sat her down and gently told her that he wasn't trying to convert her to atheism and that he was merely trying to help her understand why he no longer believed. When she heard that he was fine with her maintaining her Christian beliefs and that he only wanted her to understand him better, the barriers that she had erected came down. While his new approach was helpful and removed some of the tension between them, it did not completely restore their relationship back to where it was when he identified as a Christian. She no longer shut him down when he talked about his beliefs, but she did not hide her disappointment in him for his apostasy. And she was outright ashamed of him for his activism on behalf of atheism. David saw himself as doing something noble in working to relieve religious oppression and bigotry, but his mother saw it differently. He recounted a particularly hurtful moment where, instead of receiving praise from his mother, she deeply wounded him:

> It was my first time ever debating on a live FM radio station in the fifth-largest market in the country. So, I'm proud, and I tell my mom about it. She listens, and she doesn't talk to me. A second week goes by, and she doesn't say anything. A third week goes by, and I finally called her up and asked, "Mom, have you heard any of the interviews?" She said, "Yeah, I listened to all of them." I said, "What do you think?" because all

> my messages were about equality, respect, love for humanity.
> "It's not a practice run. Leave a positive legacy. Treat every-
> body with respect and equality"—those are my messages. . . .
> Her response probably is the single most hurtful response
> anyone has ever said to me in my entire life. I said, "What do
> you think?" She said, "Well, I just wish they would stop using
> your last name."

Bewildered, David opined that he could not understand why, even though they disagreed on the existence of God, she would be so ashamed of him, given the many worse things he could be involved with. He wasn't dealing drugs or participating in sex trafficking, but he felt his mother perceived his atheist activism as the moral equivalent of those things. It frustrated him that she could not see his point of view, which was that his work had a noble purpose. That someone he loved and cared so much about thought he was hurting society by his work pained him. He longs for her to be proud of him and what he is doing on behalf of atheism, but he doesn't expect it to happen. He found some consolation in the support he received from other deconverts who discovered his radio show or podcast on the Internet. Their support means so much to him because his mother is ashamed of people knowing his last name. His mother has been so ashamed of his work that at the company where she works, none of her coworkers know she has a son who has a radio show, has been in multiple television shows, has written a book, and has been featured in a movie. Many of them do not even know she has a son.

Some mothers attempted to win their children back to the faith. Charlene's mother debated with her over the merits of the arguments for God's existence. Frank's mother subtly tried to encourage him to find a Christian girlfriend, hoping that would solve the problem. Even though she never tried to force him to go to church, she wanted to make it clear to him that she doesn't like that he no longer goes to church and wonders what she did wrong. Marcus's mother did not seem to be overly upset at his deconversion, partly due to the fact that he was not raised in a home where Christianity was emphasized. Nevertheless, she, too, made nominal attempts to get him to reconsider his position. His mother still tries to challenge him about his atheism. She does so in a playful manner and without any animosity, but at the same time, there is truth in her jesting. She would prefer if he were not an unbeliever.

Fathers

In pointing to negative social consequences, it is interesting to note that deconverts did not mention their fathers as often as their mothers. When they did speak of the impact that deconverting had on their relationships with their fathers, they reported that the impact was milder than it was on their relationships with their mothers. Fathers were portrayed as being unaware of what was happening in the spiritual lives of their children. When they became aware that their children were wrestling with faith or actually deconverting, their responses ranged from mild disappointment to moderate support. Only in one case was there a serious attempt from a father to reconvert his child.

"My dad? I don't even know if he knows or not," said Wayne, when asked how his father responded to his deconversion. One reason Wayne gave for his father's ignorance is that they rarely seemed to talk about spiritual matters. Their conversations were limited to more mundane topics, such as business and house maintenance. Unlike Wayne's father, Steve's father did take an interest in his son's spiritual life. However, since he divorced Steve's mother and remarried, he and Steve have had little interaction. Steve has never come out to his father and identified as an atheist, but he wonders if his dad knows that something has changed due to how Steve responds to his father's wanting to pray for him. Once when he was talking to his father about a serious issue, his father asked Steve if he could pray for him. Steve reluctantly allowed his father to pray for him but was concerned about how his father perceived his obvious ambivalence to spiritual things. He speculated that if his father did find out about his loss of faith, his father would assume he was just going through a phase and that he (his father) could pray him through it.

Douglas's father has come to terms with his son's deconversion. He was not happy or supportive of Douglas's work in advancing the cause of atheism, but he did support Douglas. An example of his support was when Douglas invited his father to attend a lecture he was giving on the myth of the historical Jesus. In his talk, Douglas systematically attacked the idea that Jesus was a historical person while his father sat in the audience and listened. After the talk, Douglas invited feedback from his father. His father said he didn't agree with any of it, but he told Douglas that he did an excellent job in how he presented it. That compliment was profoundly meaningful to Douglas, and it told Douglas that, despite his deconversion, his father loved him.

Only one former believer, Tim, reported that his father actively tried to reconvert him. He affectionately described his father as the type of person who would, given the chance, start his own church. He went on to joke that his father is the kind of person who, given the opportunity, would turn any conversation into a sermon. When Tim revealed to him that he no longer was a Christian, he was surprised at how well his father received the news. He ventured to guess that it was because of his age at the time. Tim waited until he was about thirty-two before he told his father. Because he was a grown man and living on his own, there wasn't much his father could do about it. But his father's relaxed attitude to Tim's deconversion did not stop him from trying to reconvert his son, a fact that Tim found endearing. "He still tries to reconvert me every chance he gets," said Tim. "I just laugh. I think he realizes that he's not going to influence my decision on this, but he tells me he's obligated to try. You gotta love that."

Siblings

The impact of deconversion on sibling relationships resulted, in most cases, in a sense of distance and/or tension in the relationships. In some cases, the tensions increased to the point that they caused deep fissures that have not yet been healed. As one would expect, the impact was felt most acutely in relationships in which one of the siblings remained a committed Christian.

Derek and his brother Clayton were very close growing up. His brother was a committed believer, holding to the veracity of the Bible. As an atheist, Derek no longer believed that the Bible was the Word of God and had shared his feelings with his brother. Clayton holds to a conservative position on the inspiration and inerrancy of the Bible. One day, Derek told his brother—who believes in the great flood—that such a belief was ridiculous. As a consequence of their ideological and theological differences, they are no longer close and their relationship is permanently strained, although at one time they were best friends. Derek still has affection for his brother and would love for him to deconvert, but he realized that it would probably split his family apart if he did, which Derek would not want to see happen.

A more extreme situation that resulted from the clash of worldviews among siblings was that of Frank and his brother, Rich. Growing up, Rich was Frank's role model. It was Rich's conversion and Christian experience that influenced Frank to also become a believer. Years later, as grown adults, Frank and Rich would clash violently over their ideological differences. After deconverting while at a Christian college, Frank began to break the news to his family. The final person he told was Rich. He described the experience as difficult. His revelation to Rich produced two notable confrontations:

> In the first conversation, I tried to explain. I said, "Okay, Rich, I'm going to explain," and I really wanted to go through the whole logical process with him. I waited a year to tell him, and finally, he was going to sit down and listen. He knew, but he was waiting for me to talk to him, so we sat down. . . . I got five maybe ten minutes in, trying to lay out the ideas. He said, "Oh, here is your problem," and he starts giving me the gospel.

Frank felt betrayed by Rich's response. Rich had no interest in hearing him, even though what Frank was telling him was meaningful to him. It resulted in Frank feeling frustrated and estranged from his brother. For years, Frank tried to model himself on his brother and was trying to share what he had discovered and learned, and yet his brother had no interest in listening to him. That was extremely upsetting and alienating to Frank. The discussion degenerated into an argument. As unsettling as that confrontation was, it would not be the last. Several years later, Frank published an article in a book and was showing it to his family at a family pool party. He and Rich engaged in a discussion that quickly got heated and ended in physical violence:

> My brother and I were talking on the subject of religion. At one point, I got up, and I kind of yelled at him, and then he said, "Don't come in my space!" I came back, and we started arguing again. Then he said, "Well, I don't think it's very ethical for an ethics professor to download movies off the Internet" (he knew I'd been doing that). And then I said, "Oh, yeah?" I got up and I said, "You know, a lot of people say it's not ethical to hide your children away. You lock them up, so that they're shielded from all external influences, even schools." He got up, and he kind of like charged at me, and I backpedaled, and I fell to the ground. He put his hands on my neck, but he didn't squeeze; he just put his hands on my neck. I was stunned, and I just cursed him down. I'm like, "What the heck are you doing?" And he kind of got up, grabbed his stuff, and bolted out the door. His wife came in to collect all the kids' things, and they left. He's never talked about it again.

Cindy's story was similar. She and her sister used to talk frequently; now, they talk only once every two to three months. Her sister no longer calls her, even though they used to talk all the time. She bemoaned that, prior to her deconversion, she and her sister spoke on the phone several times a week, and sometimes even several times a day. Now, when they do speak, Cindy's sister doesn't talk about her religion on the phone. Their relationship has continued to deteriorate to the point where Cindy felt that her sister began to talk to her like a fool even though her sister doesn't have a college degree or even a high school diploma. Cindy tried to educate her, but she refused to look at the literature that Cindy had given her. According to Cindy, "She won't read anything but the Bible."

Spouses

As one might imagine, the relationships between deconverts and spouses experienced significant negative impacts as a result of one of the spouses deconverting. In all cases, it produced worry about what the believing spouse would think. A few marriages have successfully managed to live with the tension that inherently exists in a marriage between a committed believer and an atheist. In two cases, the marriages could not endure the tension, and they were dissolved.

The impact of Dale's deconversion was disastrous on his marriage. He and his wife grew up in the same small town and attended the same Baptist church. At the time of his deconversion, both had been moving toward a more theologically liberal viewpoint but were still committed to the core tenets of Christianity. Dale was exposed to the writings of Richard Dawkins and found convincing his argument for why it was highly probable that God does not exist. He wrestled with the argument for several days, thinking it through on his own and becoming convinced that Dawkins's conclusion was correct. Two days later, even though he still had no idea what it would ultimately mean, he knew enough to know that this wasn't something he was going to change his mind about. He had deconverted. His loss of faith was something that he briefly kept from his wife, but he did not feel comfortable doing so for long. After he revealed to his devout wife that he no longer identified as a Christian and considered himself an atheist, the marriage deteriorated. He confessed that, for several months, he tried to regain his faith and went to marriage counseling, trying to keep it all together, but in the end, he just couldn't keep it together and his marriage dissolved. It was clear to him he wasn't going to find his way back to Christianity. It also became clear that his wife was not going to continue to try to make their marriage work. After two months, he moved to Las Vegas, giving up any hope of either returning to the faith or reconciling with his wife. It was, he said, "the lowest point of my life in terms of how I have felt about myself and work."

Christopher and his wife were able to manage the differences in their worldviews, but it was not without tensions. Christopher had already deconverted before he and his wife met. His wife understood what he believed, and she herself was having questions and doubts about her faith. She was the daughter of a pastor and attended church every Sunday before they met. Although he would have liked to see her deconvert, he surmised, she would have never left the faith, because if she had, it would have been tantamount to walking away from her family. A possible reason for the lack of significant tension in the marriage was due to the fact that Christopher was already an atheist when they married. There was no sense of betrayal due to one of the parties renouncing their faith after the wedding. However, a sense of betrayal was exactly what Martin was afraid his wife would feel as he began questioning his faith. Both he and his wife were involved in pastoral positions at church, and he was moving toward agnosticism. As he thought about how his wife would respond, he wondered whether she would leave him. In the end, she did not leave him, and she became an agnostic herself. Her deconversion relieved the worry and concern Martin had had, and he reported that his marriage is a lot better today, post-deconversion, than it was when they were in ministry.

Perhaps the most unique experience in terms of how deconversion impacted marriage was that of Dave. Unlike the other participants in the study whose marriages were negatively impacted, Dave's marriage was salvaged by his deconversion. Dave and his wife dated for five years, were married for about six years, and then divorced. His wife already had a son from a previous relationship who Dave met when the son was eight months old, and he helped raise him until he was eleven or twelve. He and his wife have one daughter together. They stayed in constant contact and shared equal time with their daughter, and he spent meaningful time with her son as well. Even though his wife was not a Christian, she was also not a secular humanist activist like Dave. His wife used his activism against him during the divorce and custody proceedings. He maintained that her attorney saw an opportunity to capitalize on this and tried to make him seem like a bad parent. Despite that, Dave and his wife remained close and, according to him, never stopped loving one another. As they worked through their differences, she began working for Dave's radio program. Through the exposure provided by Dave's activism, she began to move from being an "aptheist," his term for an apathetic atheist, to an atheist activist. She is now the bookkeeper as well as the outreach director for the radio program. They are also reunited. Dave summed it up this way:

> It's phenomenal! We are back living together, and our daughter is here, and our son is here. Because of how busy I was, she didn't get the whole reason why I was an activist. But, ironically, it's also what helped to repair the relationship because we found so much common ground in helping others, in reaching out to others, in raising money for charity through my organization, and in helping a local senior center. We help kids go to science camp and do fundraising through our listeners. We found common ground there and she started to see why I do what I do. Now we share this passion, and we both do it full-time. So, we are not only back together and happier than we've ever been, but we are working towards a common goal as full-time activists, so it's been great.

Friends until the End?

For deconverts, friendships with those who remained committed Christians were difficult to maintain. When they left the faith, many reported the severing of friendships with Christians. In all cases, it was the Christians who ended the relationships. Clearly, some Christian friends felt that their deconverted friends had betrayed either them or the faith. With others, the believing friends seemed to feel threatened by the views of the deconverted. Some relationships ended gradually due to individuals withdrawing from their Christian communities. Others ended abruptly, as Christians lashed out at their friends for leaving the faith. Regardless of how friendships with Christians ended, the losses of friendships and the experiences themselves were acknowledged as negative impacts of deconverting.

Mitch's relationships with some of his Christian friends became particularly negative due to the fact that they chose to bring up his deconversion. Martin's post-Christian experience was hard because people he thought were friends suddenly turned on him. The distance Kristen experienced between her and her Christian friends may have had something to do with her geographical move away from them. But she could not help but wonder if that just made a convenient excuse for why her Christian friends no longer call her. Sam complained that, virtually immediately, many people in the church ostracized him. Rachel also felt like she was abandoned by the church. She speculated that it might be due to her divorce and her deconversion, which were simultaneous. She did not hold it against her former friends because she compared it to how people often respond to the death of a spouse:

> When a spouse dies or someone in the family dies, people don't know what to say. Then they don't say anything at all. So, I kind of feel it was part of that, too, so I don't want to necessarily say they all left me and stopped being my friends. It's probably a mixture of a lot of reasons.

The way in which friendships with Christians ended tended to be very impersonal. Few encountered direct, personal confrontations. When friendships did end, they, more often than not, did so because of natural causes, such as no longer sharing the same social space with Christian friends anymore. An interesting phenomenon that emerged from the data was an approach used by Christians to end friendships with deconverts without having to personally confront them about their losses of faith—unfriending on Facebook. Charlene experienced this approach from one of her longtime friends, Carolyn. Charlene had led Carolyn to Christ when they were in high school. They attended church and youth group together. Charlene surmised that her deconversion was upsetting for Carolyn and that she unfriended her on Facebook for a while because she couldn't deal with it. They have since reconnected and restored their relationship. Christopher had a similar experience. His best friend unfriended him on Facebook because Christopher was posting too much disturbing material about aspects of science that seemed to be at odds with the teachings of the Bible.

One of the worst experiences among participants was that of Martin. The responses from a large number of his friends were particularly harsh. One woman was very hurt and shared with him how she felt. She posted a mean-spirited letter on his Facebook wall, expressing her thoughts. Martin recounted it as follows:

> I had one lady on Facebook, out of the blue, post on my wall that she wished I never came to work at the church and that I never existed. She said I was a horrible person, that I should have never come around and I should just leave everybody alone. It just took me by surprise that somebody would say something like that. I had known her for so long, and we had a close relationship. Then, just out of the blue, she said, "You're a terrible person because you're an atheist! It doesn't matter that you're an upstanding citizen with the same wife all your life, and you've been married for ten years with a son. You're still a horrible person. I wish I didn't know you and wished my kids didn't know you, and I wished you never existed!"

The person who spoke most passionately about the losses of friendships and how they negatively impacted him was Dale. His experience was punctuated by the fact that the losses he experienced were often the result not of his friends feeling abandoned or betrayed, but of how they viewed atheism and atheists. He said the people in his life, including his family, his wife's family, and his friends that he had known since middle school, had similar reactions. He went on to clarify their reactions by sharing an experience he had with old friends who reacted negatively to his coming out as an atheist:

> I had two friends that I had in middle school, one that I am still reasonably close with and one that was kind of an acquaintance. They pretty much found out and told me that

they don't want anything to do with atheism. Yeah, I had a number of people that I would describe as acquaintances that said some equivalent of the line, "If you don't believe in God, I don't know how I can trust you."

It turned out that it was not just his old Christian acquaintances who no longer felt that they could trust him. He began detecting a pattern among even some of his closest and dearest friends, as they responded in similar fashions:

People would say "I don't know how I can trust you," and they were honest words. . . . People were treating me differently, people were trusting me differently, you know, even when I had known these people my entire adult life and had honest, intimate relationships with them. It was different after that change.

The confessions that his friends felt they could no longer trust him was shocking. Dale offered a guess at why it is that his friends did not find him trustworthy just because he no longer believed in God:

Just knowing that you believe in a God means you still think of consequences for lying, cheating, and all of these things, and they could intellectually identify that as a motivation. So, they said, you know, "But, without a God, what motivation have you got to ever be honest or selfless?" And so, they projected those beliefs upon me and those views upon me and said, "We don't think you are trustworthy anymore."

While it was troubling, Dale did not find the loss of trust particularly hurtful in most cases, because, as he said, many of the individuals who distanced themselves from him he wasn't particularly close with anyway. However, in the case of his father-in-law, his mentor when he was in high school and still a Christian, the loss of trust "cut deeply":

I kept in touch with him when I was in college much more than he did with his daughter, who I ended up eventually marrying. When he said he no longer trusted me, that was particularly hurtful. We had been through a lot together. He had been a mentor to me. We had a long history of intimate trust in our actions, so when he said to me, "I can't trust you the way that I did because I don't know that you would be honest anymore," that was particularly hurtful.

Communities of Faith

Former Christians not only lost their faith, their family, and their friends when they deconverted—they also lost the communities of faith they were once part of. All the former Christians I spoke with had, at one time, been involved in church and other Christian groups, such as college Christian clubs and youth groups. For many, it was their primary source of social interaction. After their deconversions, all of them eventually migrated out of their faith communities. In doing so, they became aware of how important being a part of a community was for them. Losing the camaraderie and solidarity that their faith communities provided was difficult and something that numerous deconverts identified as a negative experience.

Douglas identified the loss of connection between fellow Christians as definitely a feeling that negatively impacted him. It apparently struck Lauren as well. She described her time within the Christian community as one of the best times in her life. She shared that, as a Christian, she and her Christian community used to go whitewater rafting, have birthday parties, and spend holidays together. They formed a core group of friends that met her need for social interaction and a sense of belonging. Her deconversion naturally occasioned a rupture with her community. The fallout was that she lost all of those connections and emotional support. She has yet to rediscover it outside the church, although she continues to search for it.

The loss of community was agonizing for Martin. As he reflected on his time embedded in a Christian community, he acknowledged that losing those relationships was extremely difficult. "Everything in my entire life was based on my church community," he said. It took him and his wife time to figure out where to find a substitute social life post-deconversion. They soon realized that finding a community outside the church was something they really didn't know how to navigate successfully. They attributed the challenge to the fact that, when one becomes a Christian, the church provides a built-in community and an immediate group of friends, so it is easy to make connections and deep friendships. Such is not the case for atheists. Shelley made that exact point when she addressed the issue of community. Although her deconversion was not without difficulty, she began to feel a sense of loss only much later on when she realized how difficult it is to find an atheist community.

Many Voices, One Message

Losing family, friends, and community was a high price to pay for moving beyond the bounds of Christianity. The experiences of the individuals who shared their stories with me bears a striking resemblance to others who have lost their faith and lived to tell the tale. Countless deconversion narratives in the form of blog posts or articles populate the Internet, not to mention the growing number of books documenting deconversions. Over and over again, they reveal the significant negative impact that losing faith has on social relationships. Unfortunately, negative social impact is just the beginning. The personal cost in terms of emotional well-being can be just as high.

CHAPTER SEVEN

PAIN AND SUFFERING

Hurts So Good

"Sticks and stones may break my bones, but words will never hurt me." I, like many others, grew up hearing that saying, usually from my mother after I complained that someone was making fun of me. What the old saying assumes is that physical pain is worse than having your feelings hurt: "Toughen up and count yourself lucky that it's only your feelings that are hurt, not your body." And yet negative words can cut deep into our psyche and produce emotional pain that, although not as visible as a broken arm, can be more painful.

A study by psychologists from Purdue University and the University of New South Wales claims that emotional pain is as real and intense as physical pain. Researchers put participants through four different experiments intended to compare the intensity and lasting effects of physically and emotionally painful experiences. In the first experiment, researchers asked participants to relive past painful experiences and write down how those experiences made them feel. Each participant was asked to record both a physically and emotionally painful experience. Participants were then asked to note how much it hurt at the time, how often they spoke of it since it occurred, and how much it hurt now. Researchers reported that negative emotional experiences resulted in higher levels of pain than physical pain. In a second experiment, participants were given a cognitive task to complete after reliving a painful experience. Participants performed worse on the task after recalling emotional pains than they did when they relived physical pains. The researchers noted, "While both types of pain can hurt very much at the time they occur, social (emotional) pain has the unique ability to come back over and over again, whereas physical pain lingers only as an awareness that it was indeed at one time painful."[1]

Sticks and stones may break your bones, but they will heal. Emotional wounds, however, can linger for a lifetime. Former believers' stories reveal that this is the case. Losing faith and leaving a community of believers not only impacted them socially on a deep level—it also deeply impacted their emotional well-being. Losing one's faith is a major existential event in an individual's life, and often the impact is emotionally painful.

Negative Emotional Impacts

Religious faith plays a major role in constructing the world of our lived experience. It acts as one of several lenses through which the world is interpreted. The religious lens shapes the understanding of every aspect of reality and is the foundation upon which a life is built, which is why losing one's faith can be emotionally difficult and disorienting. The individuals who spoke to me shared a number of negative impacts of losing faith and becoming atheists. First, they identified an emotional vertigo that accompanied their losses of faith. Second, they identified a variety of negative emotions and feelings that resulted from their deconversions. Third, they commonly referred to two particular negative emotions that they struggled with after leaving Christianity: depression and loss.

Researcher Karen Ross interviewed former fundamentalist Christians for her study on the psychological effects of leaving Christianity, and she noted that a significant negative emotional impact is that

---

[1] Chris Irvine, "Emotional Pain Hurts More than Physical Pain, Researchers Say," *The Telegraph*, August 28, 2008.

individuals feel the acute loss of a deep and meaningful relationship. Many former believers describe their deconversion as akin to losing a close confidant and intimate friend. One participant who felt she had a deep and abiding relationship with God before she no longer accepted the truth claims of Christianity still felt the urge to connect with God despite the fact her mind told her he did not exist. She described it by using the metaphor of how she related to characters in her favorite television show. Although she knew the characters weren't real, she had watched the show so many times she felt as though they were part of her life. Likewise, because of her years spent cultivating an intimate relationship with God, she felt the urge to pray to and worship him. However, she kept reminding herself that she needed to let that urge go and live according to what she had come to believe was true, regardless of how that felt.[2] Derek's faith had been the most important thing in his life, but his deconversion made him feel like his whole belief system was pulled out of him and left him without a foundation to stand on. Douglas shared a similar experience:

> There was about a year where I knew that I was an atheist, I just couldn't accept it. I couldn't believe it. I felt like I had been flying on a plane, and the bottom had dropped out, and I was still flying. I couldn't believe what was holding me up. I just felt naked and out of my shell for about a year or so. There was a year of unsettled feeling. That was weird. I felt like a snail out of its shell. It was a weird feeling of vulnerability, I guess, is the best way to say it.

Dale's experience was similar to Douglas's in that he, too, felt the disequilibrium that Douglas spoke of, but, unlike Douglas, he didn't despair but looked forward to his expanding horizons. He never felt that life was pointless, but for several months, he had no idea what the point of life was. However, throughout that time, the one thing that made him feel better was exploring his new reality and looking for answers.

---

[2] Karen Heather Ross, "Losing Faith in Fundamentalist Christianity: An Interpretative Phenomenological Analysis" (PhD diss., University of Toronto, 2009).

Perhaps Shelley summed up the difficult and disorientating experiences of many participants best when she described the impact of losing one's religion as like being on a roller coaster of emotions.

Negative Emotions

Anne's deconversion was instigated by a discovery she made in an Old Testament class. Even though she described her deconversion as logical and rational, it still caused her to feel upset and angry and produced a lot of heated conversations with her pastor. It was difficult for her because, for the first time in her life, she wondered if Christianity was really true or if she had believed a lie. When she finally concluded that the Bible wasn't the Word of God, she said it felt traumatic and horrible. She cried because she felt like she had been completely deceived. Even though she felt angry about being deceived, it was still difficult for her to let go of her faith. She described it as terrifying and lonely. Charlene also spoke of the difficulties of losing her faith and the emotional pain it produced. When asked about her deconversion experience, she shared that the process leading up to it was difficult, and she acknowledged that she experienced a variety of negative emotions. She elaborated by saying:

> I can't really say when my doubts first began. It certainly wasn't a simple matter of, one day, no longer believing. And yet, my path from Christian to atheist can, in some ways, best be described as a conversion experience. In reality, it took years of painful, sometimes excruciating, struggle as I slowly awakened into reason.

Intense anger was the emotion that best described Lauren's deconversion process. She was upset at how she was treated after all that she had invested in her Christian community, only to be rejected by that very community. She also mentioned that alongside the anger was a deep sadness resulting from the thought of trying to replace the community she lost. She felt dejected over trying to find another group with which she fit in. Marcus's deconversion was marked by a reclusiveness at school. He stopped talking to people in order to avoid letting them know about the inner struggle he was experiencing. Perhaps a reason for his reclusiveness can be found in the observation made by Tim, who commented that, for him, what caused his negative feelings was the realization of just how much religious activity takes place in society all the time, and that it's only when you walk away from it that it's noticed. "When you do," said Tim, "then the world gets a little colder." Trina felt the coldness, too; however, the forty-five-year-old Angeleno described it as feeling like being an alien from another planet.

A somewhat surprising impact of deconverting was the feelings of frustration and embarrassment that it produced in Frank regarding his sex life. He was convinced that Christianity had stunted his sex life to such an extent that when he left the faith, his lack of experience in the bedroom left him feeling angry and resentful toward Christianity. He felt ill-prepared for sexual relationships with women who were more experienced than himself. Speaking candidly, he said:

> At twenty-three, you're dealing with people who've been going through this emotional learning curve and the sexual learning curve for eight to ten years. People your age have a good eight to ten years on you. No one is waiting to have sex 'til twenty. Even the people who wait, they don't really wait 'til twenty. So, you have this issue of how do you fit with these people? And what happens is, every time you have sex, they know. They know you're new, and it kills you because they ridicule you, or you fear they are going to. You can't deal with beginner issues because now you're behind them, and that's very crippling. And the fear of that is more crippling than anything. This is my deepest source of bitterness. And it's really, really been the most devastating impact on my life. It impacted sex and my love life. I just never had normal relationships.

Loss and Depression

The two dominant negative emotions mentioned by deconverts were loss and depression or sadness over losing their faiths. When they deconverted, they felt that an important part of their life was lost or missing, and it caused them to experience feelings of sadness or depression. When Lauren remembered the Christian community she had been a member of, it produced sadness over everything she had lost when she deconverted. For Anne, Charlene, Douglas, and Wayne, it was the missing emotional security that believing in God provided that produced negative emotions. Anne explained, "I think what has really scared me is the idea that there's not someone who is actually watching over me, and that really frightened me."

Charlene observed, "Although I no longer believed what I'd been taught as a child, I still felt like I was missing something." Douglas echoed Anne's comments about losing a feeling of security that came with belief in God. He missed having a worldview that provided him with the security of a divine God who was watching over him all the time.

Wayne also felt the absence of security and protection that resulted from his deconversion:

> I remember the first time I got on an airplane after I acknowledged to myself that I am an atheist. I remember that, at that moment, I normally had prayed. I prayed for the safety of the flight, but I remember I don't have that now. Like, I have to trust engineers and maintenance people and weather—that's it. If any of those things let me down, there's nobody who will change the outcome of this. So yeah, I missed that.

A momentous loss, such as one's religious faith, can be the catalyst for deep sadness and, in some cases, depression. Donald described his emotional state after his deconversion as "depressed":

> I became depressed for about a month afterwards. . . . I made the announcement just after Thanksgiving, and for the next three weeks, I realized I was completely uninterested in stuff

that I usually like to do. . . . My appetite wasn't really much.
I didn't really feel like talking to people, even though I was
meeting up with people regularly because everybody wanted
to talk.

As mentioned, Dale attempted to retain his faith for the sake of his marriage but was unable to. He moved out of state and started his life over
in Nevada when it became clear to him that his wife wasn't going to
continue to try to make the marriage work. For her, the assumption was
that they had two radically different religious beliefs and that a marriage
couldn't be built on two different foundations. Dale was heartbroken
over the fact that his marriage had unraveled, which compounded the
loss and sadness he felt about no longer identifying as a Christian.

All former believers who said they felt sorrow or loss from their
deconversions cited immediate and personal reasons for feeling the way
they did. For some, it was the loss of friends and community; for others,
the loss of the security provided by the existence of the Christian God;
and, for one, how Christianity negatively affected his sexual development. Only one person identified feeling depressed as a result of the
logical consequences of atheism. Marcus astutely observed that one of
the consequences of atheism was that humans do not have any ultimate
significance. The realization that he and the rest of humanity were not
the creations of a loving God but the result of Darwinian evolution
initially was hard for him. "Since I don't believe that each human being
is inherently special or anything like that, I guess that is depressing
sometimes, but it's not really something that keeps me awake at night
or anything like that," he said.

It is not surprising that deconverting from Christianity to atheism
produced a variety of negative emotions. However, what is most striking is that only one participant identified losing his relationship with
God as a source of negative emotions. When asked if they missed being
in a relationship with God and whether losing that relationship caused
any sense of loss or sadness, only Wayne responded in the affirmative.
"Yeah, I mean, I regard it as like a loss of friend," he said.

Meaning, Purpose, Value

Psychiatrist and Holocaust survivor Viktor Frankl once said, "He who has a *why* to live can bear almost any *how*."[3] Frankl's point was that if a person can discern meaning in the midst of suffering, they are much more likely to be able to endure it. One of the benefits often reported by religious devotees is that their faiths provide an ultimate meaning to human existence. Moreover, it provides a why in the midst of the ubiquitous suffering of human existence. A belief in God not only infused life with ultimate meaning—it also ensured that suffering was not in vain and that, despite all appearances, it had a purpose in the good and wise plan of God. When one deconverts, they not only give up on the existence of God but, consequently, any ultimate meaning to human existence or the hope that evil and suffering have any redeeming values. Such losses are not small consequences. Each deconvert had to deal with the effect that adopting atheism had on the meaning and purpose of life. Although former believers recognized the loss of ultimate meaning as a negative consequence, it was not, however, a debilitating one; most were able to come to terms with life not having a grand meaning.

Anne admitted that, when it comes to reality, there is no deeper meaning to life. Her belief is connected closely with her view of origins; that is, she believes that humans are a species that evolved to perpetuate life. Tim offered a similar response to the question of meaning in an atheistic universe. He suggested, "We're lucky to be here. That makes sense of it. There is no bigger reason, there is no bigger meaning, there is no higher power. The reason why we're here is because we're here."

Marcus echoed the views of both Anne and Tim and traced his view on the meaninglessness of life to his view on human nature. As an atheist, he no longer believes that humans have the inherent dignity and value that he once believed they did in virtue of being made in the image of God. He acknowledged that when one gives up on their belief in God, they also must give up their belief in inherent human value and, thus, in an ultimate meaning in life. The consequences of the loss of those

---

[3] Victor Frankl, *Man's Search for Meaning* (Boston: Beacon Press, 1992 [1959]), 88.

two things were mildly depressing for him. As mentioned previously, Marcus concluded that when he lost his faith in God, he concluded that the only account of human origins that was left as an option for him was Darwinism. But since, according to that theory, humans are the products of natural selection operating on random, beneficial mutations, there was nothing ultimately special or valuable about humans. Therefore, although it was a depressing thought, Marcus acknowledged that when it comes to meaning, value, and purpose, none of those concepts apply in any objective or ultimate way to humans.

Like Marcus, Donald felt what he referred to as a big void for the first couple of months after he deconverted. He attributed that to stepping away from his purpose in life for the past thirteen years. When asked by friends how he can make it in life now that he no longer believes in God, he honestly replies that he doesn't have a satisfying answer. He elaborated by adding, "Christians say, you know, 'I live for Jesus, I want to serve Jesus, I want to bring people to Christ.' I don't have a simple answer to that. . . . I'd be lying if I gave you a clean, clear answer."

Mitch repeated similar thoughts. He confessed that, in his work with palliative care patients, he has observed how his atheist patients struggle with the lack of having a purpose in life. He went on to affirm that if people don't have a purpose in their life, it is detrimental to one's psyche. He, like Marcus, realized the connection between the image of God and human value and meaning. Now his views on human origins are that we all come from stardust. Looking at it that way for him has been a big blow to what he referred to as the narcissism that humans have concerning their place in the universe. However, Mitch realized that, even though there is no ultimate meaning to life, atheists must create their own meaning. "Basically, if you don't have a purpose in life as an atheist, you have to create a purpose. I am perfectly okay with that." Although he accepts that, as an atheist, he must create meaning in life, he admits that it's no easy task. "You have to make purpose in life, and that's definitely a struggle."

Karen Ross discovered similar findings. One of her participants, Stan, became distressed upon coming to the conclusion that God doesn't exist. He echoed author Fyodor Dostoyevsky's claim that if God does not exist, then anything is permissible. It seemed entirely consistent to him that he could steal, kill, and rape, because there is no ultimate accountability. Unlike many other deconverts, Stan seems to grasp what many philosophers, both theistic and atheistic, have claimed regarding the relationship between God and morality, which is, without God, there is no objective foundation for morality. This led Stan to become depressed that the world was falling apart. Given that the only other viable origin story once he left creationism behind was that of Darwinism, Stan concluded that humanity was no different from bacteria in value—it was only luckier. For Stan, no God meant no morality and no meaning.[4] Ross's findings are consistent with my own. Consistently, former Christians report that losing their faith had the effect of turning their world upside down. For some, everything felt pointless, meaningless, and insignificant.

While most former Christians admitted struggling to varying degrees with the loss of ultimate meaning for human existence, Dave saw it as liberating and exciting. He, too, believed that life has no ultimate meaning, so one must create it in order to stave off existential anxiety, but he expressed no sense of remorse over that fact:

> When you realize that you are equal and you are all growing together, you realize that that's the beauty of life and that your meaning of life is to discover your meaning. Your meaning of life is to find your purpose. The purpose of your life is what you make it to be. You are truly in charge of your own destiny, and that is not only extremely exciting but incredibly liberating. I have no predetermined set of laws, and I don't follow ABCD that I could go to this place and I can't go to this place. It's not a test; it's not a quiz. I'm in charge, and I could leave a positive legacy and do something phenomenal in my life, or I can sit in front of the television and not make an impact— that's okay. [If] that's what I choose to do, that's okay.

---

[4] Ross, "Losing Faith," 135–36.

Ross also uncovered three other negative emotional experiences that are typical of deconverts. First, they feel the loss of their identity. This should not be surprising, since for evangelical and fundamentalist Christians, being a Christian is not an add-on to one's identity—it is the core of who they are. To be a follower of Jesus is to lose one's life in his service by taking up one's cross and following him. To say that Jesus is Lord means that he is the king of one's life and that the individual no longer is the captain of their ship. All things are interpreted through the lens of "What would Jesus do?" or "What does Jesus think?" Consequently, when that foundation is swept away, it can be disorienting. Deconverts can struggle to understand who they are apart from their relationship with God.[5] They are then left with the task of reconstructing an identity, but doing so apart from any set of established doctrines or communities proves difficult. I suspect that it's the need to rediscover who one is that has led to the proliferation of unbelieving social groups that can be found online.

The second negative emotional experience typical of deconverts is the loss of comfort and hope. Again, this should not be surprising, given that individuals have left a worldview that offers unconditional love from a God who has a vested interest in them in this life and is waiting for them in the next. Furthermore, it is not only the hope of eternal life that deconverts lost, but the hope of reuniting with loved ones in heaven. Under their new set of beliefs, when their loved ones die, they cease to exist, and the hope and comfort of seeing them again is gone. Acknowledging that is the case often proves troubling to former believers.[6] For others, the sense of loss goes beyond the fact that this life is all there is. Several former believers expressed a sense of hopelessness with life in general. The absence of the providential hand of God over their lives was acutely felt.[7] Prior, when they were believers, the belief that God exists and is orchestrating events in the world and their lives to his desired end brought with it a comfort that helped them endure

---

[5] Ross, "Losing Faith."
[6] Ross, "Losing Faith."
[7] Ross, "Losing Faith."

difficult times. Now, for some, getting through even the humdrum of a normal day is a challenge in terms of having a hopeful outlook, let alone when things get hard.

The third area in which Ross discovered negative emotional effects from deconverting concerns loss of direction.[8] No longer did deconverts feel that their lives were being guided by God. During their Christian period, former believers felt that their lives were directed by God to accomplish his greater plan for the world. This made prayer a meaningful exercise because prayer was a means of seeking God's will and an avenue through which God revealed his will. But in losing belief in God, former believers lost any overarching structure to their life. Moreover, life became unpredictable, unstable, and, worst of all, the responsibility of the individual. No longer was there a right path to take in order to arrive at a destination that is uniquely set by God; there was no path to discern. As one participant put it, "There's nothing to figure out. Like, you're just gonna do whatever you're gonna do with your life, so, good luck."[9]

Based on her findings, Ross makes an insightful observation about the nature of negative emotional experiences associated with deconversion. She points out that the losses are intertwined with each other. For example, she maintains that loss of meaning and direction intensifies the loss of identity, and vice versa. Of particular interest are Ross's observations that former believers recognized that the Christian story was beautiful, fulfilling, and valuable, despite the fact they no longer believed it to be true. Perhaps this is why she concludes that by acknowledging what they once believed and the positive emotional support it provided them, "their personal reactions of grief, depression, or disappointment—whether recalled or demonstrated through tone or tearfulness—revealed that unbelief came at a high cost."[10]

---

[8] Ross, "Losing Faith."
[9] Ross, "Losing Faith," 139.
[10] Ross, "Losing Faith," 140.

Paying the Price

We began this chapter by looking at the old saying, "Sticks and stones may break my bones, but words will never hurt me." Not only is that saying false; it is predicated on the assumption that physical pain is worse than emotional pain. From what we have seen, I suspect that deconverts would beg to differ. They testified that emotional hurts are not only painful but also deep and long-lasting. All former believers spoke of experiencing strong negative emotions as they deconverted. Feelings of anger, confusion, depression, sadness, and loss were associated with losing their faith. Individuals also said a negative impact of their deconversions was the loss of an ultimate meaning in life. Some still wrestle with that loss and actively fight off the encroaching nihilism that they feel. At the same time, some have come to terms with it and believe that the loss of ultimate meaning in life has imbued this one life they have with more value since it is the only one they will ever have, and they are determined to make the most of it.

CHAPTER EIGHT

STRATEGIES

Strategic Initiative

I live in Los Angeles, California, and if you know anything about Los Angeles, you know that it suffers from two things: intolerable traffic and the constant threat of earthquakes. According to the California Earthquake Authority, there are more than one hundred active fault lines near Los Angeles and a 75 percent chance of a magnitude 7.0 (or greater) earthquake in the next thirty years.[1] The consequences of such an event could be disastrous, which is why the State of California and local governments encourage residents to have plans in place to mitigate the damage. We are told we need strategies in place to help us cope in the event the "big one" hits. So, many of us have stored food and water, stocked up on medicine, purchased earthquake survival kits, and anchored heavy furniture items to the walls. My family knows that if we are at home and an earthquake hits, we need to get under a table and wait for it to stop. Then we need to find each other. I will shut off the gas, do a quick check to make sure the house is structurally safe, and find a safe place to shelter in the event of aftershocks. We also have a strategy to communicate with

[1] "Los Angeles Earthquake Prediction—What Is LA's Risk of Getting Hit?" *California Earthquake Authority* (blog), April 21, 2020.

each other if we are not at home and an earthquake happens. My point is that an earthquake can cause major damage and that it is important to have a strategy that will help lessen the impact.

As we have seen, leaving one's faith, like experiencing an earthquake, can have significant negative consequences. Earthquakes destroy buildings and break bodies, whereas deconversions can destroy relationships and emotional well-being. And just as Angelenos have strategies in place to deal with the negative consequences of earthquakes, deconverts put into action various strategies in order to offset the negative consequences of losing faith. This chapter highlights the three strategies former believers utilized for dealing with the impact of their deconversions: (a) how they chose to reveal they were now atheists, (b) how they chose to live their lives as atheists, and (c) how they engaged with Christians post-deconversion.

Strategy 1: How They Revealed Their Identities

Former believers realized that how they revealed their identities to others had the potential to negatively impact themselves. In order to avoid negative consequences, they used two opposite strategies. First, they sought to avoid negative pushback, and they cautiously revealed their atheist identities to trusted friends and family. Second, they were not as concerned with the negative consequences as with taking an open stand for atheism.

Cautious approach. Knowing that identifying as an atheist could have negative consequences caused a number of deconverts to mitigate the impacts by coming out slowly and cautiously. For Mitch, it was a slow process of deciding what he wanted to tell people. Some of his summer camp friends know that he doesn't believe anymore. On the whole, he has chosen not to reveal the change in his worldview to many of his friends. Martin confessed that although he has been an atheist for some time, it wasn't until recently that he started posting articles on the Internet and letting people know where he stood on Christianity. Recounting to me the journey to publicly declaring her identity as an atheist, Kristen spoke about the fear that can be generated by identifying as an atheist. Due to her upbringing, embracing the label of atheist produced fear, resulting in her identifying first as an agnostic until she was ready to come out as an atheist:

> I would probably say at some point I called myself agnostic because I think I'm too scared to call myself an atheist just because of the upbringing, just because of the way atheists were stigmatized for me as a child. I was taught that an athe-ist is the worst thing a person could be. You could be a lot of things but being an atheist would be pretty bad. I could handle the term *agnostic* but not *atheist.*

Likewise, Christopher also refrained from calling himself an atheist, concerned about what others would think. He began calling himself an atheist only in the last few years. He, too, was afraid to come out and identify as an unbeliever. The reason he was scared was because of how he used to treat atheists when he was a believer. A second fear that kept him from identifying as an atheist was the lingering fear of hell. He knew, according to his old worldview, that he was now destined for hell, and that if his family was correct, he was in trouble. Sam believes it's easier for apostates to self-identify as agnostics than as atheists. On one hand, it's motivated out of epistemic humility. On the other hand, it is motivated out of fear of how they will be perceived if they claim the label of atheist:

> I think the majority of people are more comfortable with using the agnostic rather than the atheist label because they don't want to say, "I'm an atheist." I guess people, in their mind, when they say that, it always implies, "I'm a Satan wor-shipper" or "I'm a pagan."

Wayne's fears were of a more practical nature. The combination of his loss of faith, his adoption of atheism, and where he lived made him con-cerned about what might happen if word got out that he was now an atheist. Being from the heart of the Bible Belt, where there is a church on nearly every corner, it's common when one meets somebody to ask them where they go to church. One doesn't have to start by asking if a person goes to church. The practical consequences he feared if it became known he was no longer a Christian revolved around issues of employment and whether or not his change in worldview would impact him financially: "I was very paranoid that it may have a financial impact on us," he said. "We have to be careful if this gets out, I might not be able to get a job, I might get fired, I might have to look for another job. It was about my biggest concern of mine at that time."

Open approach. While some of the individuals took their time and were deliberate in whom they confided their loss of faith, others were more open. They chose to deal with the impacts of their deconversions by facing them head-on, come what may. In general, they wanted people to know about the changes in their lives and were more than happy to declare them openly in different forums.

Martin posted on Facebook in order to help others who might be going through difficult times as they matriculated through the deconversion process. Initially, he was cautious, but he soon decided that the benefit of assisting others was worth it. It took him a long time before he worked up the courage to do so, and when he did, he decided that he wouldn't attack religion but instead send the message to others that it's okay to be an atheist. In return, he received a sense of solidarity from others who liked his posts. He hoped that he too could provide comfort for other atheists living in places where atheism is a minority view and one that is often looked down on.

Unlike Martin, who took his time to identify as an atheist, after his deconversion, Marcus quickly came out as an atheist on Facebook by updating his profile. He wanted everyone he was friends with to know his new religious views. However, shortly after his initial post, he removed the label from his profile because he didn't want to limit the people who might want to talk to him based on his atheism. Even though he didn't believe being an atheist was something that should earn him the cold shoulder from friends, he was aware of the potential for that to happen.

Shelley was even more outgoing in her public identification as an atheist. Not concerned about what others thought, she actively engaged in attacking religious ideas as a means of identifying as an atheist. For a period of time, she went through what she described as a militant phase, constantly bashing religion. She was careful not to attack religious people, but she aggressively attacked religious ideas. Not concerned about what others think of her atheism, she is content with people challenging her or accepting her for who she is. When they do challenge her, she responds by engaging them in dialogue that sometimes becomes confrontational. She's okay with that because she believes that some ideas are so bad that they deserve no mercy.

Wayne pursued a similar strategy of revealing his deconversion by going public on the Internet and actively seeking out Christians in order to engage in dialogue. Immediately following his deconversion, he was hungry to debate the toughest opponent he could find. He emailed a couple of people that he knew who were committed Christians and well-versed in their faith, and he shared with them that he was now an atheist. He then invited them to have a discussion with him. His intention was not merely to engage in interfaith dialogue. He was intent on demonstrating that Christianity was false and harmful.

Strategy 2: How They Lived

Once they had let it be known to friends and family that they were no longer Christians but, instead, atheists, former Christians were faced with the question of how they would live as atheists. Given the stigma attached to being an atheist in the United States, how each answered that question revealed a particular strategy for dealing with the potential impacts. How individuals chose to live out their commitments to atheism differed according to each person; however, as in the previous section, two distinct approaches were discernable.

Diplomats. The first approach former Christians adopted in living as atheists was a diplomatic one. They were concerned about avoiding needless tension and causing unnecessary offense in the way they lived out their atheism. For these folks, although atheism is an important part of who they are, it's not something they feel should cause strife if it can be avoided. To be clear, being a diplomat should not be understood as being embarrassed or shy about their beliefs. All of the former believers were forthcoming about what they believed and were more than happy to talk about it. Nor should being a diplomat be understood as a reflection of their commitments to atheism. All the individuals were committed to their denials of the existence of God, and some of the most diplomatic in the public presentation of that denial were the staunchest nonbelievers. Diplomats seek to avoid potential problems by not raising the issue of atheism. This doesn't mean that they never talk about it or get in heated discussions; it simply means that they let the battles come to them and do not seek them.

Charlene, while living in Virginia, interacted regularly with Christians who assumed that she, too, was a believer. Given a choice between engaging them in conversation, which potentially would risk damaging relationships, and remaining quiet, she chose to remain quiet and let them continue on in their assumptions. She explained:

> In Virginia, people would talk about their Bible study and
> morning prayer, etc., assuming those around them agreed or
> did the same (on the school playground for example), and I
> just listened. Growing up with that, it's not unfamiliar, and I
> understand that it's important to them and don't feel a need
> to attack them.

Charlene was able to navigate successfully in both worlds, that of her personal worldview and the dominant socioreligious worldview in the area in which she lived. By choosing to listen only and not share her views, she retained her friendships, which, for her, were more important than changing their minds about the existence of God.

Charlene related to her mother in the same way that she interacted with friends in Virginia. A devout believer, Charlene's mother has endured watching all six of her children turn from the faith in which she raised them. As she was going through her deconversion, Charlene used to debate with her mother. They have since come to an agreement in which they no longer discuss religion because it's too upsetting for both of them. While she used to hide her convictions from her mother, she no longer does. Charlene was content for her mother to believe in God and no longer desires to challenge her faith. "God works for her, and that's great," she stated. As a diplomatic atheist, Charlene was more than willing to share her views but saw no need to disabuse others of their beliefs as long as they held them graciously. Commenting on a particular religious belief that she did not accept, she expressed her attitude of tolerance:

> I just can't believe that God is real because if he were, I couldn't be where I am today without him, but here I am nevertheless. People wouldn't be able to find peace any other way, but they do. And it's not the same for everyone—some people truly believe in reincarnation. If that helps them deal with life, I say, "Go for it," as long as they don't push their beliefs on everyone else.

Douglas is also a good example of a diplomat. He acknowledged that there are different approaches that deconverts utilize as they live out their atheism. He didn't believe that there was any right way to do so, and he felt no compulsion to tell others what the best way was. He pointed out that in any movement or ideology, there are in-your-face adherents, and while that may be okay for some, it wasn't the way he had chosen to live out his commitment. He did acknowledge that there are certain people who choose to flaunt their beliefs and take an in-your-face approach to interacting with others. He has chosen a different approach, but at the same time, he is not shy about sharing his beliefs. If someone tells him something he disagrees with, he is quick to let them know how he feels. What makes Douglas interesting is that he is a well-known atheist activist. He is an author, conference speaker, and national organizer of numerous atheist and humanist events. He is a leader within deconverted circles and is widely known and respected for both his winsome character and ability to articulate his position.

Douglas is an excellent example of the fact that atheists can be both diplomatic in their approaches to atheism and be advocates. He is clear in his commitment to atheism and would not avoid confrontation if it were to come his way, but he doesn't seek confrontation for its own sake.

Concerned about what people might think about her deconversion, Kristen was quiet about her loss of faith. Interestingly, her concern wasn't what people would think of her, but she was concerned to not hurt or offend Christians. She clearly saw that any attempt to explain why she was no longer interested in church inherently had the potential to offend somebody. Not wanting to offend others created a difficult decision for her and her husband. When friends and acquaintances discovered they had deconverted, she and her husband were faced with a dilemma. They could say nothing and let people assume the worst, or they could explain their reasoning and worry that their friends would feel that expressing their thoughts was an attack on their faith.

Realizing that she could not control how others would respond to her loss of faith, she took consolation in the fact that other atheists and agnostics have faced similar experiences, and she drew peace from having a sense of solidarity with them. "I do expect some people will make very wrong assumptions about the choice to leave Christianity, but, once again, that is something we just have to accept and move on and take peace in the fact that other atheists and agnostics get it."

Another example of a diplomatic deconvert is Mitch. Committed to the nonexistence of God and happy to dialogue with anyone about it, he felt no compulsion to evangelize. In contrast to the authors who so impacted his own deconversion, he took a more supportive role toward those who were in the midst of their journeys, as opposed to attempting to actively deconvert Christians. If a Christian were to come to him sharing their struggle, Mitch would not try to convert them to atheism. Instead, he would listen attentively and share his own story. If the individual decided they no longer believed, Mitch would be happy for them, but it would not be his goal. After his loss of faith, Marcus sought to identify with others of like mind and attended college. He visited gatherings of prominent secular and atheist campus clubs for social purposes. However, the tenor of the clubs was such that it did not fit with his way of living out his unbelief. As a diplomatic atheist, the strident tone of the campus clubs was not appealing to him. "Yeah, I've been to a couple of meetings. I don't know, I just didn't really enjoy being there, because a lot of it was bashing Christians and groups that we didn't agree with. So, I stopped going there after visiting twice."

Firebrands. Firebrands typically seek change and are willing to engage in activities to that end, even if it angers others. For example, Steve is motivated to wake people up to what he sees as the dangers of religious faith. He isn't trying to antagonize believers when he challenges them about their beliefs. On the contrary, he sees what he is doing as analogous to unplugging people from the Matrix.

An unexpected discovery of the strategies used by firebrands was that some shared the further motivation to change the views of other atheists. Firebrands believe, and according to studies, they have good reason for doing so, that atheists are viewed by the general public as amoral and untrustworthy individuals. Their activism is directly tied to changing that point of view. Dave, a full-time humanist activist, is a prime example of someone who chose this strategy. After his deconversion, he quickly came to the conclusion that Christianity was not only false—it was also dangerous. Shortly thereafter, he was mentored by a prominent atheist who gave him guidance and opportunities to advocate for atheism and humanist causes. Today, Dave is the host of a popular radio program that broadcasts for three hours daily, attracting 160,000 listeners per month. The show is dedicated to secular causes, advocating for atheism, and challenging the truth claims of religion. Renouncing belief in God also led him to reject belief in the afterlife. This caused him to turn his focus to this life and to actively making it better for himself and others. He has chosen to do so by becoming a secular humanist activist. For many, losing belief in God produces a sense of personal vertigo regarding who they are and why they are here. Dave eagerly desires to spread the word that this does not have to be the case:

I had the goal of creating heaven on earth, creating my paradise here. I'm going to do it because I want to create a comfortable living environment for myself. It's about not infringing upon other people. It's about loving one another and realizing that you are part of something bigger than yourself. This desire to believe in a God because you always felt like there's got to be something bigger starts to go away when you start to embrace atheism. But, once you embrace humanism and secular humanism as part of your atheism, the belief in something bigger comes back.

One way that Dave sought to change people's views of atheism was to change their views of atheists themselves. He did so by publicly identifying as an atheist, then by living a life he believed would challenge people's presuppositions of atheists. One way he chose to do that was by having the word "ATHEIST" on his license plate:

People are constantly taking pictures of the license plate. I see it all the time, starting conversations behind me in the car. But it's my way of showing that atheists are not black holes with black fingernails and long black hair that you can push into the closet. It's not equal to gothic; it's not equal to Satanism or anything negative. It's a short, chubby, bald guy in a Ford F-150 who is taking his daughter to school. Atheists are regular people who are not out to hurt you. I will let you in traffic; I'll wave you over. I will let you walk across the street without running you down. And people see this on a day-to-day basis, me acting humanly and civilly in society, just like everyone else, with this branding of atheism on me. And, that's what I do. I don't do it to start a fight; I don't do it to push it in anyone else's face. I do it to let them know we are everywhere.

Jill, like Dave, chose to adopt an open-and-out-there strategy in expressing her atheism. For her, an important principle that needed to be retained was the separation of church and state. Feeling that Christianity often was given a pass on violating that principle, she chose to take a stand against religious expressions that cross the line. In the years since her loss of faith, she has become more active in how she lives out her atheism. She put a stop to the town sponsorship of the Christmas tree lighting. In response to the nativity scene and the nativity play the town had sponsored, Jill protested that it violated the separation of church and state because the play took place on public property. Even though she believes people can worship however they want and set up as many nativity scenes as they would like on private property, she would not stand for it on public property. "When you're violating the constitution, doing it on public property with public sponsorship, I have a big problem with it," she said. Her activism spurred on another woman to take up the mantle on behalf of activist atheism. She shared that "a local woman who is a member of a local atheist meetup group contacted me, and she came to support me, and it inspired her to contact the Freedom From Religion Foundation to set up a local chapter. So, she got inspired to start a chapter because of what I did." Jill's work was not only centered on stopping the encroachment of religion in the public sector; it was also concerned with changing the views others have of atheism. One way she went about doing that was by partnering with the Freedom From Religion Foundation in organizing a billboard campaign in her hometown. The purpose of the campaign was to change people's perceptions of atheists:

> We had a billboard campaign here in San Jose. Just a group
> of atheists coming out with billboards saying, "Hey, we are
> people, we're real people like you. We're your neighbors, your
> friends, your coworkers. We just happen to not believe in
> God." So, we did this billboard campaign—very positive, and I
> was on two of them, and it was in the newspaper.

Referring to the story of a young Muslim woman who had suffered greatly for her deconversion, Mitch commented, "I am going to start sharing that I am a deconvert myself." His primary reason for doing so was to add to the projects of other atheists who were "trying to reduce the idea that we eat babies."

Firebrands not only seek to change how people view them and atheists in general; they also actively seek to aid each other as they live in a predominantly religious society. That means organizing atheist social groups in order to facilitate the need for community and atheist political groups directed at bringing about changes in the law in order to benefit atheists. Tim has created social spaces for atheists and political action groups. His purpose was so new atheists could have a safe space to come out of the closet. He built a local freethinkers' group for a few years and also created a number of atheist conventions. He is now actively involved in a secular community that meets every week with nearly thirty people—this acts as a social gathering for unbelievers. Concurrent with his work in creating events and communities for atheists, Tim also has goals of being politically active. His focus is on social activism, and he is willing to work with religious groups in order to bring about positive changes in the community:

> And I'm in the process of starting an atheist group that will
> have more of a social activism direction. The secular commu-
> nity is just a place where people can get together, eat, drink,
> and discuss whatever they want in a taboo-free environment.
> If you want to talk about God stuff, that's great. If you want
> to talk about movies or shoes or politics, that's cool, too.
> Primarily, we just want nonbelievers to know that they're not
> alone. At the same time, we will be more active in terms of
> being active in the community, raising money for local causes,
> promoting dialogue and being in cooperation with religious
> organizations in the area. We are trying to get the community
> to see that we're not baby eaters.

It's interesting to note that what motivated him in doing good was not exclusively the benefit he can provide others but also that it will reflect positively on atheists. Like other firebrands, he is concerned about the misguided views people have of atheists.

Strategy 3: How They Engaged Other Christians

Deconverts once identified themselves among the faithful; they were embedded in churches, Bible studies, parachurch organizations, and Christian clubs. For many deconverts, the greatest pushback they received was from those they left behind as they detached from various Christian communities. One approach that several deconverts used, when criticized, was to go on the offensive and turn the tables on believers. Tim's method was to challenge faith in the Bible. When people who tried to argue with him started with the Bible, he responded by asking them questions about the trustworthiness of the Bible—questions like "Where does the Bible come from?" and "Who wrote it?" One of his favorite things to do was to challenge the authorship of the Gospels by maintaining that they were written by anonymous individuals, not by those whose names they bear. If they could prove their beliefs to him, he was open to agreeing with them. But he wasn't holding his breath that that would happen anytime soon. Mitch reasoned with believers by appealing to the fact that both he and they don't believe in many of the same gods. Neither he nor the Christians with whom he was conversing believed in the gods of Greek or Roman mythology, or even the god of Islam, for that matter. So, he argued, all are atheists to one degree or another. However, he had chosen to deny one more god than they did:

> One thing that I've tried to do is to point out that Christians
> know what it's like to be an atheist. Every single person in
> this room knows exactly how to be an atheist towards Islam,
> or toward the great God of the oceans, or whatever. You all
> know exactly what that feels like. That is exactly what it feels
> like to be an atheist; we've just gone one god further.

Shelley shared an encounter she had with a believing friend concerning faith healing. According to Shelley, they were talking about religion and sharing their perspectives. Her friend challenged Shelley with what she assumed to be proof of God's existence. Her friend recounted the story of how the elders of her church gathered together to pray over a man who had cancer. When one of the elders emerged from the prayer time, he was holding a large black mass in his hands, and the man no longer had cancer. Shelley was quick to point out to her that what was being offered as evidence for God's existence was, from Shelley's perspective, not impressive at all. Instead of merely accepting the story and avoiding conflict, Shelley challenged the entire story. She labeled the story as ridiculous and charged the people involved as charlatans. She poked several holes in the story and showed that the evidence in support of the healing was flimsy at best. That was the last time Shelley spoke with her friend. Although she was disappointed, she added that even though she lost a friend, she accomplished her goal of challenging at least one believer to think.

Following a New Playbook

In order to mitigate the impact of deconverting, participants revealed that they knowingly or unknowingly engaged in certain strategies. This chapter identified three strategies that featured prominently in the data. In the first instance, participants were careful how and to whom they revealed their deconversions and their new identities as atheists. In the second instance, participants were inclined to adopt one of two stances in relation to how they lived their atheism publicly. Some chose to be diplomats, while others chose to be firebrands. In the third instance, participants utilized various methods to engage Christians in post-deconversion dialogue. This primarily consisted of engaging them in argument in order to show that Christianity was false. Usually, this strategy did not meet with positive results. And yet, in terms of their deconversions, former believers don't lack what they consider to be positive results. It is to these cases that we now turn.

CHAPTER NINE

FREE AND CLEAR

Free Falling

For two years when I was pursuing graduate studies, I worked as a window washer. My boss operated a residential window-cleaning company, and he and I traveled throughout Southern California, cleaning windows. He did the outside of the windows and I did the inside. Doing the inside of the windows meant that I needed to go in each home, which often resulted in having a chance to meet and chat with the owner. I met many interesting folks doing that job. But of all the people I met over those two years, there is one I will never forget. Her name was Olga. She was in her late eighties and lived with her husband in a nice home in Yorba Linda. As I walked up to her house to wash the windows, she stood at the door and welcomed me in. Her body was frail, but her voice and Eastern European accent were strong. After exchanging initial pleasantries, I asked her where she was from. "Poland," she said. I told her that I had visited Poland a number of years ago and that my grandfather on my mother's side was from Poland.

"How long have you lived in the United States?" I asked her.

"Since 1945," she said, "the year the Russians liberated me from Auschwitz."

Stunned, I blurted out, "You were in Auschwitz?"

She rolled up her sleeve to show me the tattoo identification number the Nazis had given her. "Yes, I was, and the day that the Russians set me free was the greatest day of my life," she said.

The desire for freedom is one of the deepest longings of the human heart. We value freedom so much that we are even willing to fight wars to defend it. When citizens commit serious crimes, we take away their freedom to punish them. The worse the crime, the longer the time they are sentenced to prison. Why don't we just fine them or make them perform some kind of community service? The answer is that when someone does something really bad, they deserve a punishment that fits the crime. Freedom is so important to us that taking it away is how we do that. There is no better demonstration of how much we desire freedom than that of US founding father Patrick Henry, who cried, "Give me liberty or give me death!" Freedom, liberation, emancipation, independence, whatever you want to call it, is one of the most desired states of human affairs. It's also the dominant characteristic of deconversion testimonies. Former believers consistently say that losing their faith set them free. And even though the cost of obtaining their freedom was high, in terms of the negative consequences we looked at previously, it was worth it—well worth it.

Free at Last!

Despite the many negative consequences associated with deconversion, deconverts consistently report that the impact of deconverting is overwhelmingly positive. Although leaving Christianity and adopting atheism was fraught with difficulties and the price they paid was high, it was clearly worth it for what they received in exchange. Believing that they had discovered the truth and, as a result, had been set free from the falsity of Christianity, provided cognitive and emotional benefits that they felt they were denied when they were Christians. Dave was clear about how deconverting impacted his life. "I really want to bring this point home," he said. "It is an overwhelmingly positive impact to go from Christianity to atheism. Overwhelmingly positive. As an atheist,

I don't feel like there's a limit. I mean, I can live my life in any direction I want to."

Others confirmed and expanded upon Dave's perspective, reflecting on how deconverting caused them to have different views of themselves. They used such phrases as: "I've grown healthier as a nonbeliever"; "I'm more pleased with myself"; "I'm more comfortable with myself"; "I relished the challenge it presented"; "I'm calmer"; "I have higher self-esteem"; "I'm more honest with myself"; "It was really exciting"; "It was a growing time"; and "It was a very blossoming time."

Positive Emotional Impacts

As individuals shared their stories, two themes emerged regarding their perceptions of the positive impacts of deconversion. They felt that deconverting produced positive consequences, both emotionally and intellectually. In terms of the way they felt and thought about the world, deconverts believed they were better off after their deconversions than before. This chapter looks at the positive emotional impact of deconverting. The major emotional theme that dominates deconversion narratives is that deconverts perceived themselves as being set free, happier, more compassionate, and having a greater sense of peace since leaving the faith behind.

Freedom

When asked what positive impacts deconverting had on their lives, deconverts responded that they were now free; altogether, the twenty-four participants expressly referred to being set free or liberated thirty-five times in the interviews. Twenty-one used the words *free, freedom, liberated,* or *liberation* to define their experiences, or they described being set free or liberated from Christianity. There was a strong sense that Christianity once bound them, but that deconverting liberated them and provided them with opportunities to flourish as people. Freedom from what they perceived to be an oppressive and arcane Christian religion came at a cost for all, but all testified that it was a price worth paying. The emotional and intellectual positives

153

THE ANATOMY OF DECONVERSION

outweighed the negative impacts. The cost of freedom was high but, ultimately, worth it.

Ex-Christians explained their liberations differently. Frank's liberation began when he picked up a book by Sam Harris, a prominent atheist. In Harris, he found someone who, like himself, felt that Christianity and religion in general were wrong and hurtful. In regards to religion, Frank said it was as if someone was finally willing to say, without fear, that Christianity was wrong and harmful, which Frank found refreshing and liberating. For the first time, he had read someone else who thought the way he did. Furthermore, he felt that his deconversion freed him cognitively from previously prohibited academic pursuits. He found freedom to read whatever he wanted without having any preconception about what the conclusion would have to be. One author who particularly impacted his thinking was Michel Foucault, who opened his eyes to the role social forces play in shaping our thinking, especially in the area of sexuality. Frank found Foucault's thinking intoxicating because of the freedom and openness that it provided him. He described the impact of deconverting on his intellectual life as follows: "My heart was just aflame for this openness to new ideas, wherever they went. I think that was extraordinarily liberating."

Wayne echoed Frank's sentiments. He, too, gained intellectual freedom from his deconversion. He became freer to question many of his previous beliefs. Now an atheist, he believes there is nothing so sacred that it can't be questioned. Similarly, Mitch found himself experiencing a sense of greater intellectual freedom after he walked away from his faith. For him, it stemmed from finding more coherence with his beliefs as an atheist than when he was a Christian. "There is like a freeing peace now that I don't have as many intellectual problems with my values system. Like I was saying, my value system I don't think has drastically changed. I think it has gotten easier in terms of congruency. It's more congruent," he maintained. Why was it more congruent than when he was a believer? Because Mitch did not feel the need to try to make sense out of doctrines that he had always felt were incoherent but that he had to believe if he were going to be a Christian. Admittedly, some doctrines of the faith are challenging. But Christians have worked hard to demonstrate that while some of what they believe is paradoxical, it is not incoherent. Nevertheless, there are some beliefs that Christians must affirm in order to be a Christian in the most basic sense. Even that was too much for some former believers. Rachel complained that Christians often told her that she had to believe certain things if she wanted to be a Christian. She found that intellectually restricting. But, as an atheist, she is happy because now she can choose for herself what she wants to believe, and she loves that freedom.

Whereas Frank, Wayne, Mitch, and Rachel's liberations came in the form of intellectual pursuits, more often than not, participants' liberations came in the form of being set free from what they perceived as the oppressive nature of their faith. During her time living in the Bible Belt of Virginia, Charlene began to allow herself to ask the question: What if there is no God? Prior to that time, she was afraid to even think such a thing. But when she did, she discovered that the world didn't fall apart. That simple question allowed her to see things in a new way. It was an eye-opening, freeing experience that liberated her from the narrow and restrictive thinking she had developed throughout her childhood. Tim's experience was similar to that of Charlene's. When he finally gave up his faith and accepted that it was behind him, he described it as having "an incredible burden that just vanished from my fundamentalist shoulders. And, the constant condemning that goes along with fundamentalism, until you get away from it, then you're like, 'Oh, this is great!'" He described his life as a Christian as burdensome because, for him, the Bible was a book that taught he was only to love the people of God and hate everybody else because they were sinners and enemies of God. Because they were worldly and living lives in opposition to God, they were to be hated. Deconverting meant that he did not have to comply any longer, which he described as a huge plus because he no longer had to live under that cloud of intolerance anymore.

Christopher no longer felt that he had to live up to an unrealistic set of expectations, nor did he care what other people thought of him. He found freedom in knowing that some people would like him and that some people were going to hate him for leaving his faith. The feeling of always having to live up to standards can be burdensome, and being relieved of that burden can provide an individual with a sense that they have discovered truth. One of the ways this happens is when former believers find that leaving Christianity frees them from the condemnation and guilt that they experienced while Christian. Numerous former believers mentioned guilt and condemnation as feelings that characterized their life as followers of Christ. For them, the church was not a place where they experienced the love and grace of God—it was a place where they had their faults criticized and their failures exposed. Never feeling able to live up to what their churches or families believed was necessary in order to be a good Christian was wearisome and discouraging. It produced a feeling of failure and low self-worth. There is no doubt that this made them susceptible to the intellectual and emotional challenges that eventually led them out of the faith. The feeling of guilt that so many former believers speak of was not only a result of being judged by those in their churches—it also was a result of how they viewed God. They tended to see God as an overbearing, angry, never-satisfied parent who was ready and waiting to criticize them when they did not meet his expectations. Losing belief in God lifted that burden and was experienced as a positive aspect of Christopher's deconversion. Where the relief was felt most acutely was in the release of guilt and condemnation he felt he lived under while a Christian.

When asked how deconversion positively impacted her life, Shelley said, "Initially, there wasn't [a positive impact], except for relief. I kind of felt like I felt free. I felt like there's nobody watching me. I felt like, I don't know, all I can think of is free."

Jill raised the issue of freedom from the fear of eternity. In the past, it was something that had caused her concern, but, because of atheism, she doesn't have to worry about heaven and hell, or whether there is judgment awaiting her after death. Deconverting emotionally liberated her from those fears, and she is now free from what she felt was the stigma and expectation that came with being a Christian.

Besides the intellectual and emotional relief discussed, a third sense of freedom mentioned by the participants was the freedom to live as they choose. Rachel found joy in the freedom to be friends with those who weren't believers. She can now enjoy unbelievers for who they are, and she no longer feels the need to evangelize them. She asserted that she was now "free to be able to enjoy people, not just for the purpose of evangelizing them or making sure they turn away from their sin and to be saved. . . . I was just able to see them for who they were." No longer was she concerned about having to decide if people are responsible for their sexual orientations or about holding that against them like she did when she was a Christian.

> Were they born that way, or did they make that choice? . . .
> When I'm at church, what I was taught was that it was the
> choice they made, not that they were born that way. So, I
> am able to see people and appreciate people without any
> thoughts of what will God think? Or God needs me to evan-
> gelize them. Or God needs me to win them, so we see them in
> heaven. And, I just get to appreciate people, so that has been
> very freeing.

Her spectrum of relationships broadened, and she noted that she is now able to have relationships with all kinds of unbelievers. She is free to talk and hang out with them, no matter who they are and no matter what they believe. Sam also spoke of being freer to accept individuals, regardless of their shortcomings. He was content with accepting people for who they are and not despising them for who they should be but are not. "I'm not trying to change anybody anymore," he said. Nor did he look at the world through the lens of us versus them or as an in-group versus an out-group mentality. As a result, his relationships with the majority of his friends improved.

Happiness

Freedom was not the only positive impact that resulted from deconversion. Thirteen individuals stated that they are happier as atheists then they were as believers. Those who didn't specifically use the word *happier* did, nonetheless, portray themselves that way post-deconversion. Repeatedly, former Christians communicated that leaving the strictures of the Christian faith produced in them an emotional state of joy and contentment. Even though the process of deconversion was difficult, perhaps the reason so many deconverts testified to being happier was because, as Charlene said, "In the end, things were better." Regardless of how difficult the journey was, the end result was worth it in the eyes of participants.

Dave gave powerful testimony as to how one could be happier as an atheist than as a believer. He no longer viewed himself and fellow Christians as a special group loved by God in a unique way. He had come to see himself and everyone else as part of something bigger than just atheists; for him, it was humanity as a whole. He felt that we are a part of one family to which we are all related to some degree. Dave saw all of life as an interconnected whole, each part related to the other through the natural process of evolution and chemical composition. Therefore, he felt a deep connection to nature. He said, "I can stand out in a forest and be moved to tears knowing the relationship my body has with the earth, that someday I will return to that." Furthermore, with the knowledge that he has a limited amount of time to live, he marvels at the fact that, given cosmic and biological evolution, the odds of him being here are astronomically small. "The fact that I'm literally made of stardust, of things from space—it is phenomenal," he said. "It's moving, it's emotional, it's sexy. It's all of these things that I can only verbalize as genuine happiness. I hate to take that long way around, but the sure answer is happiness." He went on to say, "I have to say there is an overwhelming improvement in my emotions, period." As a consequence of accepting his place in the universe, he continued:

> When I do something for someone, it is not because I think that God is watching. It's not because I'm trying to rack up points for heaven, or because it's a Christian, or Muslim, or Jewish thing to do. I simply understand that all humans are

connected and not only in an evolutionary and biological
way, which is cool in itself, but also in a bigger part of humanity. So, it feels really amazing that we are part of this giant
moving body of humanity, that I get to play a role in that. So, I
am extremely happy.

Dale's transition from Christianity to atheism was precipitated by an
intellectual problem. It was decidedly not because he was unhappy,
which is why, for him, it made it all the more surprising that his deconversion produced greater happiness. He adamantly denied that he chose
atheism. He became an atheist because he agreed with an argument,
and he didn't know what else to do. What he discovered, to his surprise,
was that he became happier and more satisfied in life than he had been
before. He eventually came to the point where he believed that, with
few exceptions, religion is a bad influence on people.

Other participants who testified that they are happier now as atheists were Sam, Cindy, and Martin. Sam said he is "a lot happier now"
that he is no longer in church, "a lot happier" since he left Christianity,
"a lot happier" not having to answer to other Christians, and "happier"
that he no longer feels the need to try and convert people to Christianity.
Cindy is also happier being an atheist and away from all the negativity
and judgment and the anti-educational attitude she believes character-
izes the church. She stated, "I'm happy because I'm away from all that. I
just felt really happy that I don't have to deal with it anymore."

Reflecting on his journey and how difficult it was, Martin shared
that, despite it all, "You know, I consider myself now . . . I'm a lot happier
than five or six years ago." Martin is representative of all the participants
I spoke with for whom deconversion was the means by which they were
able to reconcile many of the loose ends of faith they wrestled with as
believers. For them, deconversion was the path to a unified self, a self
no longer at war with itself. Looking back over their journeys, they
identified the result of finding that unity of self as happiness. When
asked what constituted happiness, former Christians spoke in terms of
binary opposites and how they now identified with the positive binary

concept, whereas when they thought of themselves as believers, they identified with the negative concept.

Compassionate versus Judgmental

Conversations with former believers, as well as print and online testimonies, reveal that deconverts drew sharp distinctions between their attitudes toward others when they were Christians and their present attitudes as atheists. They uniformly testified that, prior to their deconversions, they were judgmental and intolerant of others who believed differently than they did. As atheists, they saw themselves as much more compassionate and open to others. No longer did they discriminate along lines of religion and behavior. When they did discriminate, it was based on what they believed to be secular reasoning, not religious faith.

Because of his difficult experiences, Frank was more open to the experiences of others, even if they were not in line with his preferences. He felt as though he stopped having the kind of myopic concerns that he did as a fundamentalist. He also stopped seeing everything in terms of black and white without any grey. Douglas became more open, and his consciousness expanded in relation to others and how he interacted with them. He spoke at length about how it changed the way he related to other people:

> Well, I felt very special as a Christian in the sense that we
> have the right answers and we are going to heaven and
> everybody else is going to hell. Now, I feel that same kind of
> specialness but not in the same way. It's not an ego-driven
> way. I feel like I'm special, and everybody else on the planet
> is special, too. And, that's really cool. What surprised me the
> most is when I stopped being the kind of Southern Baptist
> that's very judgmental, I was able to look at people in a
> whole new way and be connected to them in a way I never
> had before. Because when I was a Christian, I was the type
> that would look at somebody and judge if they were saved or

not. "Oh, they're Baptist, they're saved. Oh, they're Lutheran, they're saved. They're Catholic, they're going to hell. They're Mormon, they're going to hell." Once I got rid of that, all of a sudden having a Christlike concern for all people was effortless. I felt more connected to humans. I felt more connected to my place in the universe and everything in a way I never had before. And I love that. I really loved that a lot.

Dave's views about others also changed for the better. His atheism cast life in stark, urgent terms that he felt demanded he treat each person with dignity and respect, regardless of who they are or what they believe. The greatest impact he saw from being an atheist was his love and respect for humanity. Losing a belief in an afterlife had a significant impact on his views about this life. He came to realize that the legacy a person leaves and the memories one leaves with others is of utmost importance. Likewise, the lessons he teaches his children and the way he interacts with people each day have taken on greater meaning. One thing he realized that had a massive impact on how he viewed living his life was the result of losing the hope of conscious existence after death. As a Christian, he treated this life as a practice run for eternity. All of his hopes and dreams were focused on eternity, and that impoverished his life in the present. But as an atheist, he is now making the best of this life because he believes this is the only life he gets. Whereas before, he restrained his behavior and curbed his desires in light of eternal rewards, now he lives fully for the earthly delights and joys that he is certain of.

That he now sees this life as his only chance to experience fulfillment has also affected his work on behalf of secular humanism. That all humans are in the same situation when it comes to having only this earthly, temporal experience has created in him a love for humanity that he described as the biggest change in his life since his deconversion. Dave summed up his views about how deconverting changed his attitudes toward others by contrasting the worst manifestations of Christianity with his understanding of atheism:

Not that all Christians are negative. . . . But the ones who
want to oppress, the ones who want to control and maintain power, they definitely use that book [meaning the Bible]
against humanity. When you become an atheist, you shed
that; you shed the negativity, the desire to oppress. You see
equality without God-goggles on; you don't feel [that] you are
specially chosen by a powerful being. You feel free; you feel
free to treat each other with respect. You don't have to hate
anybody, and it's a positive viewpoint of humanity.

Other former Christians raised the issue of judgment and intolerance
being associated with Christianity. Anne, for example, believed that she
was more tolerant as an atheist than as a Christian. She also indicated
that she was more empathetic now than when she was a Christian. Not
only was she more empathetic, but she also believed she was less judgmental as an atheist than as a Christian. Drew affirmed that, for him,
losing his faith made him more open to accept people for who they were
and where they were coming from. He became more concerned about
asking others what he could do to make their life better than he ever
did as a Christian. His concern was no longer for their eternal destinies
and whether they were in the Christian community, but how he could
increase their present happiness and reduce suffering. He claimed:

I think I am less judgmental than I was. I remember coming
down pretty hard on people in high school. "All the Bible," I
thought, "they should follow the Bible." I was pretty dogmatic
when I taught Sunday school, so I think I was one of those
pretty ugly Christians, unfortunately. So, I think I'm less judgmental than I was back then, less black and white.

Rachel felt strongly that, since her deconversion, she had been liberated
from judgmentalism and intolerance. She spoke of the constant tur-
moil that she experienced as a Christian when she tried to hate the sin
and love the sinner. Now, as an atheist, she is able to appreciate people
for who they are and love them for what they are without having to

judge them for their behavior. She no longer feels pressure to change the attitudes, beliefs, or behaviors of others because God doesn't like what they are doing. She feels a great sense of relief that she no longer needs to correct others out of loyalty to God and his Word. She grieves, in hindsight, that, as a Christian, she felt that she was disrespectful to those who believed differently. Deconverting has provided her with a greater sense of self-awareness. Now that she is no longer a believer, she looks at herself from a different perspective. When she was a Christian, she believed that she was disrespectful of people who didn't believe the same way she did. She claimed that as an atheist, she doesn't do that any longer. As an atheist, she is interested in what people believe, how they feel, and why they feel that way. She is now

> able to embrace people as they are right now, no matter who they are, no matter what choices they have made. I have more friends who are homosexual. I appreciate them as people and what they have to offer in life and am not necessarily worried about what sexual orientation they are. I know as a Christian, when I was one, what we are called to do is to love everyone. And now that I am out of that, I don't think a lot of people really did that. I think as Christians, if we really were sup-posed to do that, like in the Bible how Jesus had said, "Love everyone," I think things would be different because I hon-estly feel that I am more loving and accepting [of] people now than I was as a Christian.

Sam, like Rachel, felt that he, too, is less judgmental as an atheist than as a Christian. He also believed he is more compassionate, caring, and freer to accept individuals with all of their shortcomings, beliefs, and preferences. Cindy, too, confessed that a positive impact of her decon-version was that she could now accept people for who they are without having to judge them. She saw herself as warmer now than before and focused on the collective welfare of others, instead of merely focusing on herself. Shelley bluntly said that her deconversion caused her to "hate less people" and become more compassionate. She felt she was more supportive and more forgiving than when she was a Christian because, as she put it, "You don't have to funnel everything through how wrong some of these other people are."

Peaceful versus Anxious

The second way former Christians explained what happiness meant was in terms of gaining peace and losing anxiety, worry, and guilt. Although losing their faith brought negative emotions, it also brought awareness of the substantial negative emotions that were the result of their faith. They shared that they often felt they were not good enough for God, that they worried about their eternal destinies, and that they felt guilt over sin and shortcomings. While it's true that they suffered some negative emotions when they deconverted, eventually those subsided and were replaced with a sense of freedom. When participants deconverted, they left behind the belief system, lifestyles, and communities that they believed produced those negative feelings. In the place once occupied by those negative emotions, participants found peace. Donald definitely felt more at peace, but he noted that when he was a Christian, he also felt peace. The peace he had acquired as an atheist, though, was different. He described it as a more mundane and ordinary peace that came with leaving Christianity behind because it was Christianity that caused him stress. Now, when he goes to bed at the end of the day, he feels content with himself and isn't consumed with repenting of all the things that he didn't do that he believed God required of him or the things that he did wrong. That was a great source of relief for him.

When Charlene allowed herself to ask about the existence of God, she noticed that the world did not come crashing down on her. Doing so allowed her to see things in a completely new way. She found it eye-opening and freeing, and it brought a peace that she had never before known. Steve found the same thing. Though asking that same question was sobering and terrifying, the intellectual freedom it provided him brought him great peace.

Others, like Wayne and Martin, found in their deconversions a relief from guilt. Wayne said, "As far as positive things, I would say I feel much less guilt. I can go to bed every night and think, 'Okay, I was honest to everybody today, did my best to help people around me, I have nothing to be ashamed of.'"

Likewise, Martin felt scared to even entertain the question of God's existence because of the image of atheists that was ingrained into him as a child. When he began to have growing doubts, he was faced with the inevitable question of whether he even considered himself a Christian. He remembered experiencing a lot of guilt over that, and becoming an atheist relieved him of that fear and guilt:

> I remember just because it was so pounded into me as a kid growing up, that atheists are bad and equated with evil. I'm really scared at first, thinking, "Should I even be question-ing these things? Do I even consider myself a Christian?" I remember experiencing a lot of guilt over that. I'm like, "You know, I don't even know how I could be thinking these things. Obviously, if I am thinking these things, God knows that. Is he mad at me?" You know, I felt a lot of that for a few years, when I started to become an atheist. I don't have that anymore. I don't have all the unnecessary guilt over my head anymore.

Reflecting on his darker times as a Christian, Frank had burdens that he felt guilt over, despite the fact that they weren't hurting anyone. This produced in him guilt over the kinds of things that made no tan-gible difference to the people in his life. As an atheist, he sees the guilt as misplaced. It was guilt over things that, in his mind, were of little consequence and did not hurt anyone, while ignoring more important issues. Instead of being worried about how his actions were affecting the people in his life, he was worried about whether or not he was having lustful thoughts. Since leaving the faith, that sort of anxiety has completely fallen away for him. No longer being a Christian has allowed Frank to be more concerned about how his behavior is affecting other people and has also freed him from the guilt that came with an overly religious conscience.

Donald addressed the issue of guilt by referring to the sense of obligation he felt to share the Christian message with others. He commented that, in the past, he felt guilty that he did not do it more or do it better. Donald said, "I feel less guilt now that I don't preach to my coworkers."

Jill no longer felt a sense of worry or fear over her own salvation. Becoming an atheist removed any concern for where she would spend eternity since she no longer believed in a conscious existence after death. She identified a liberation from worry as a positive impact of deconversion. She maintained that, because of atheism, she doesn't feel any loss at all. On the contrary, she feels liberated that she doesn't have the fear and worry about an afterlife, about heaven and hell, and about the judgment the Bible speaks of.

The person who spoke most about guilt and the freedom that atheism brought was Sam. In commenting on how he now lives his life as a nonbeliever, Sam tries to do the best he can for other people. One of the ways he does that is by being respectful to others. As a result of living by those maxims, he maintains he experiences less guilt than he did as a Christian because there is no one keeping track of his failures. One specific example he gave was in regard to his friendships with gay people. As a Christian, he was always concerned that if he were seen with his gay friends, he would be rebuked. As an atheist, he no longer needs to care. He no longer has that guilt, and he doesn't care what anyone thinks when he chooses to go out with his gay friends. Today, a lot of guilt about spending time with non-Christians is gone for him. In summarizing his deconversion, Sam said that he was much happier now and free from guilt. But it was not an easy road to being set free from his sense of guilt and shame. Yet, for Sam and the other participants, it has, according to them, been worth it.

Free Agents

The sense of emotional freedom and happiness that resulted from leaving the Christian faith is not the only positive outcome of deconverting. Former believers also testify that, after their loss of faith, they experienced a greater ethical and epistemic improvement as well. Put another way, they became convinced that how they previously went about determining right from wrong and what is factually the case was woefully inadequate when they were Christians. Deconverting afforded them a different epistemological and ethical paradigm with which to approach life. No longer bound by ecclesiastical pronouncements or commands from the Bible, they were set free to follow other sources of knowledge, which they found enlightening and liberating.

CHAPTER TEN

ENLIGHTENED

Be Reasonable

Immanuel Kant is widely regarded as one of the most significant phi-losophers, if not the most significant, of the period in western history known as the Enlightenment. The Enlightenment, or what is sometimes called the Age of Reason, was both a period of time and a movement that reoriented the political, philosophical, scientific, and religious bearings of Europe in the eighteenth century. In 1784, Kant wrote an essay titled "What Is Enlightenment?" in which he described just what is meant by the word. In his essay, Kant asserted, "Enlightenment is man's emergence from his self-imposed tutelage."[1] For Kant and other Enlightenment luminaries such as Locke, Voltaire, Diderot, and Hume, the goal of the Enlightenment was to be intellectually set free by using one's own reason to evaluate the reigning orthodoxies of the day and the authorities who enforced them. "'Have the courage to use your own understanding' is the motto of the Enlightenment," wrote Kant.[2] What

---

[1] Immanuel Kant, "An Answer to the Question: What Is Enlightenment?" in *Perpetual Peace and Other Essays*, trans. Ted Humphrey (Indianapolis: Hackett, 1983 [1784]), 41.
[2] Kant, "An Answer to the Question," 44.

that meant for Kant and other thinkers is that individuals, and the public in general, needed to throw off the shackles placed on them by the guardians of knowledge and use their own reason to determine what was true. Nowhere was this more important for Kant than in religious matters. According to Kant, submitting oneself to religious authorities rather than using one's own reason to determine the truth was "not only the most harmful but the most dishonorable" way to arrive at beliefs.[3]

The Enlightenment, then, was seen as an intellectual coming of age. Through the use of reason, humanity would grow into maturity and be set free from the fetters of dogmatic authorities. In short, Enlightenment thinkers believed that tossing aside religious authority and dogma as the sources of knowledge and truth in exchange for the conclusions of reason would bring freedom. Deconverts would heartily agree. Besides experiencing a sense of emotional freedom and happiness as a result of their deconversions, former believers testify to being set free ethically and epistemically. Like their Enlightenment predecessors, deconverts have also come to believe that religious claims are "not only the most harmful but the most dishonorable" way to determine the truth.

Positive Intellectual Impacts

Deconverts uniformly view their deconversions as positively impacting what and how they believe. Specifically, they pointed to the impacts that deconverting had on their ethical beliefs and their criteria for determining truth claims. Like the positive emotional impacts of deconversion that produced a sense of freedom from the confines and strictures of Christianity, participants spoke of a freedom, both explicitly and implicitly, in relation to the intellectual impacts of deconversion. Intellectual freedom is understood to be a new approach to ethics and knowledge. This section presents findings that make it clear that deconverting affected former Christians' morality and shifted the criteria by which they determine the truth from revelation to reason.

---

[3] Kant, "An Answer to the Question," 44.

Ethical Improvement

It is often argued or even assumed that unless a person believes in God, they either cannot be moral or have no foundation for morality. Deconverts are quick to challenge both of those assertions. In fact, most believe that they are more ethical as atheists than they were as Christians. That self-perception is due, in part, to their changes of mind over what is a morally prohibited action. As this chapter will demonstrate, deconverts not only changed their minds on the nature of the relationship between God and morality, but they also changed their minds on moral issues.

Ethically better. Dave's morality changed after he lost his faith, but he had no doubts whatsoever that it had changed for the better. Although it has not changed much in his day-to-day interaction with others, it has changed dramatically in relation to his overall worldview. He observed that he finds within him an overwhelming desire to give back and leave a legacy by reaching out and helping those in need. What motivates him is the solidarity he feels toward others who he has a shared biological connection with. As an atheist, he recognizes that there is no God who will step in and provide a miracle cure for a disease or the funds to buy a much-needed wheelchair or lifesaving medical procedure. The onus to meet those needs falls on humans, and that realization has motivated him to take up many causes on behalf of others that he would never have when he was a Christian. Why? Because back then, he would have waited to determine if it were God's will for him to get involved. Instead of taking a proactive approach to social issues and acts of mercy, he would have waited on God to somehow instruct him that he should get involved. If God didn't give him a sign, then he took it as God's will that he not get involved. Today, as an atheist, he feels he has no one to pass the blame onto for his apathy. This motivates him to do what he can for other humans who he looks at as incredibly precious individuals with whom he shares the "miracle" of existence. In his eyes, and contrary to what many Christians assume, losing his faith has not made Dave less moral but more moral.

Like Dave, Frank believes he became more moral as a result of his faith exit. For him, it was in becoming more compassionate. The reason why is because he was no longer seeing everything and everyone through the lens of what the Bible taught. This, he claimed, allowed him to be open to everyone on their own terms. He was clear that losing his faith has not robbed him of many of the virtues that he valued while a Christian. Honesty is still important to him. And despite being what he called a pushy person who wants to argue, he believed he approached issues with a new ethical openness, as opposed to the closed stance he had as a believer.

A common analogy used by deconverts is that losing their faith is a lot like growing up. That is how Dale likened the change in his ethical perspective. He maintained that children need instruction until they are mature enough to make wise choices on their own. Dale compared his former life as a Christian to that of a child who needed ethical instruction from a parent figure—in his case, God. As he matured, he came to believe that God was no longer needed to tell him how to act ethically. Nor was he acting ethically merely because he was told to, but because he was choosing to, because of informed reasons:

> It felt like growing up. It felt like, when I was a kid and a mom said, "Don't hit, don't lie, share your toys," those kinds of things. I didn't really feel like I had all the answers, but early on . . . I had [the] feeling of "I'm now no longer doing these things because somebody tells me they are good. I am now doing things that have a more fundamental meaning of good to me."

He freely admits that not having God or the Bible to appeal to did make ethical decision-making opaquer. There were fewer clear answers to moral dilemmas than before, but all of that does not seem to bother Dale. He found that feeling he is growing up morally was a step in the right direction, whether or not he ever gains clarity on many moral matters. One thing he is sure of was that when he does get clarity, it will come from thinking carefully, not by special supernatural revelation:

We just do the best that we can, and so a lot of the answers to moral questions felt to me like I was forced to say, "I don't know, and I'm not sure if I'll ever know." But the reasons that will compel me will not be dogmatic ones. It went from that to seeking out what I think is best and most healthy. And I get to answer those complex questions to the best of my ability. That felt like growing up to me. It felt like I stepped in a positive direction.

Lauren's departure from the faith caused her to reflect back upon her time in the church and the unethical and immoral practices she believed she perceived. As previously mentioned, she wrote a scathing indictment of church ethics where she compared the acceptance she received from the adult film industry to that which she received from the church. She maintained that the truly loving community was not the church but the adult film community. There, she perceived more acceptance for who she was than within the church community. Since leaving the faith, she believes that, if anything, her morals have gotten stronger, part of which she credits to learning about acceptance and compassion from those in the adult film industry! Even though she no longer believes in God or an afterlife, she suspects that if she is wrong and it turns out there is a heaven, she would probably end up there. Her reasoning is that all she ever wants to do is help people, a trait she learned not from the church but from the porn community.

Mitch tended to believe that although his ethical stance had changed since his deconversion, it hadn't changed much. He hadn't begun to frequent brothels or use drugs. He hadn't become a degenerate gambler or a contract killer. What had changed, however, was his reasoning for not doing any of those things. Even though he was not going to brothels, he would no longer have a problem with someone else patronizing them. He's open to other people engaging in behaviors that he would not. He no longer thinks that morality is as absolute as he once did when he was a Christian. Back then, if something was wrong, it was wrong for everyone. Now he's much more relativistic. While he doesn't think going to brothels is right for him, he has no qualms about someone else going to them. He's even open to the possibility that later in life, when he's at a different stage in his journey, he will change his mind on the matter. This more open, tolerant, and accepting attitude Mitch sees as morally superior to the closed, intolerant, and exclusive attitude he had when he was a Christian. Furthermore, he also thinks that jettisoning Christian morality has brought more coherence to his belief system. No longer is he trying to intellectually justify biblical injunctions about how to live that never made sense to him.

Biblical morality. Deconverts tended to see themselves as more moral since their deconversions, citing their shifting view of the Bible as a major driving force in their lives. Former believers raised questions of the morality found in the Bible and found it difficult to understand how Christians could base their approaches to ethics on such a troubling text. From the dark stories of how God dealt with the inhabitants of Canaan to potential inconsistencies, deconverts did not find much moral worth in the pages of the Bible.

For example, Charlene's problem with the Bible and the idea of God is that they give people a sense of moral superiority. But that sense is just an illusion since, ultimately, appealing to the Bible doesn't really solve anything because, like all documents, it must be interpreted, and interpretation is always based on a host of presuppositions that impact the received meaning. That being the case, saying that something was wrong by appealing to the Bible, according to Charlene, was similar to looking down a well and seeing one's own reflection:

> The Bible is full of inconsistencies and is open to interpretation, which is why there are so many different religious groups, even within Christianity. People have to pick and choose what they believe and still have to come to terms with their own moral values. Christians can say that their beliefs are based on God's teachings and feel comfort in knowing that they are right for that reason, but it really just gives a person a way out of tackling the tough issues for themselves.

Sam supported Charlene's observation about the Bible being a poor source for deriving one's ethical system. He, however, was even stronger in his condemnation. He believed that the Bible advocated and even prescribed many moral atrocities, such as slavery and incest. And yet not a single Christian today will say that slavery is good. Not a single Christian today would say that pedophilia is good. Not a single Christian today would tell you that murder is okay. But in the eyes of Sam, all those things are not just acceptable in the Bible but promoted.

God and morality. It is sometimes said that, without a belief in God, persons cannot be moral because God's existence is a necessary precondition for moral behavior. Such a belief, however, is misguided. There's no reason that an atheist cannot be a moral person. The real issue is whether or not an atheist can provide a satisfactory account for the existence of objective moral values and duties without postulating God's existence. Regardless, a question that many deconverts reported being asked after they left the faith was how they managed to remain moral individuals, given their atheism. Unsurprisingly, deconverts disagreed with the concept that, without belief in God, it's impossible to be moral. They all consider themselves fairly moral people, and they don't believe in God. What is interesting is that not only do they think morality without God is unproblematic—they came to the conclusion that the real problem belonged to Christians. How could they justify their belief in objective morality required by God when the God they based their morality on was the God of the Bible who, in their mind, was obviously an immoral monster? Furthermore, many developed an alternative account for ethics. Ethics, rather than being some kind of transcendent law weighing down on us and authored by a moral lawgiver, was much more mundane. They regularly pointed in one of two directions to account for the existence of moral obligation: common sense or evolution. Jill argued that one does not need God in order to have morality; all one needs is to think rationally about it:

> I'm a good person, and I know that I'm a good person,
> because I think it's good to be a good person, and I believe

in morality and ethics in doing the right thing. And, I never felt that I had to do it because God is telling me to. I find that very, very tragic.

Charlene concurred, and, after losing her faith, she slowly learned that she did not have to believe in God to be a good person. Knowing that it's not right to kill, that you shouldn't take anything from your neighbors, that it's healthy to rest, are all a matter of common sense for her.

The whole idea that morality required God was foolish for Sam. He argued that one does not need the Bible to tell us how to treat each other; one does so because it's obviously the right thing to do:

> For me, it's another reinforcement that you don't need Christianity to be a good person. I don't need Christianity to tell me that it's a good idea to be a good Samaritan or to help others in need. I think the difference is that now I realize that Christianity doesn't have the exclusive "Love thy neighbor." They really like to think so, and they presented it as though it's impossible for you to love your neighbors as yourself, that it's impossible to do good things without the Church. I think that, you know, I can be a good person, I can be a wonderful person without the Church.

Tim had a similar point to Sam. Although he appealed to animals as an example of sentient beings that do not believe in God but still exhibit social empathy, he didn't explain the moral sense by way of evolution. He simply asserted that such moral knowledge was hardwired into both animals and humans. He categorically rejected the idea that, without the Bible, humans would be just like animals. He even argued that animals have social empathy. Many species, especially higher mammals, like apes, take care of their own. They defend them from outsiders, and they take care of their young according to the instinct within them. Morality, for Tim, doesn't come from a verse; it comes from a kind of common sense that's just part of who we are as human beings.

Evolution and morality. According to natural selection, mutations within species that provide a survival or reproductive advantage will be selected naturally. Selection, in this case, implies that creatures with positive mutations will survive and pass on their genetic material. All aspects of biology can be accounted for in terms of natural selection acting on beneficial mutations over time. In the atheist account of reality, there is no room for nonmaterial substances, such as God or the soul. Therefore, morality is not a transcendent law existing outside of humans but merely a sense that aided our ancestors in surviving. Deconverts who seek to offer a theoretical account of morality frequently appeal to evolution, perhaps because it's the only option that they have. An example of how deconverts do this is shown by Martin, who argued that people have evolved to be moral. Over time, we have come to realize that it's good for us to not kill each other. Conversely, it's good for us to be kind to each other. We have evolved to appreciate peace and harmony, and the instincts and moral sense that we possess push us in those directions. Those basic instincts were, according to Martin, part of our makeup prior to the development of religion, so they cannot be the result of religion. He summed up his view as follows:

> My idea of where moral values come from now is different. I think it is an evolutionary trait; we just know we are better off not trying to be selfish and going out and hurting and harming other people. That's not a good thing. You're going be cast out from a community if you do something like that.

Cindy also appealed to evolution to explain why it is that we have empathy. She argued that we evolved with empathy, and she maintained we learned from the consequences of actions. "I mean, if I kill somebody, obviously I'm not going to feel very good; I could go to jail. If I rape somebody and I do drugs, I'm destroying my health. There are consequences to everything we do, and I want to be happy. That's what I want, so the good thing is to be happy." In other words, morality isn't an objective set of values and duties that she's beholden to. It's a sense that has evolved within humans that helps us avoid negative consequences and negative feelings.

Two Main Issues

As one would expect, deconverts expressed that they changed their minds on numerous moral issues. However, two issues were prominent: abortion and sexual ethics, specifically homosexuality. In terms of abortion and homosexuality, participants reported that they no longer believe the same as they did when they were Christians. Also, they were clear that their changed positions on the issues were indicators of moral progress.

Abortion

Dave admitted that, if he were a Christian still, he would have to be against abortion based on the principle that the baby is "God's child." However, since he no longer believes in God, he is no longer bound to view the child through the lens of faith. His current view now sees a baby through the secular lenses of the principle of individual autonomy in combination with the "property-thing" view of human persons. The property-thing view of personhood is a metaphysical doctrine that holds that a human being becomes a person only after it accumulates certain properties. The property-thing view stands in contrast to the substance view, which holds that a person is not determined by the successive addition of properties, but by its essential nature. Christians tend to hold to a substance view of identity and maintain that a baby is a person from conception, based on its essential nature, not that it becomes a person only after it acquires a property like sentience.

Dave thought the logic that Christians used against abortion, even in the case of rape, to be fundamentally flawed. If life is so God-ordained, why would there ever be a reason to end a pregnancy? Even more, Dave offered a startling case study about bodily autonomy. He imagined what would happen if a person causes a traffic accident and injures another driver. In his scenario, the driver is hurt to the point that they need a new kidney, and a matching kidney is found. It turns out the driver who had caused the accident was a perfect match. Dave then wondered:

> If I crashed into you, and it was completely my fault, and we were the same blood type, and we are a match for a kidney donation, and you were going to die, and you needed a kidney to live, and I caused your pain and suffering, and I was a perfect match for you, there would still, never, be any law that would require me to give you one of my kidneys because we still respect bodily autonomy.

He then noted that a pregnant woman should be able to decide whether or not to share her uterus with a fetus, just as a person might choose to share their kidney in a theoretical life-threatening situation. "You can't grant the same body autonomy to two joined humans," Dave argued, "and that fetus is not yet a fully developed human, so I feel like the woman should have more rights than the fetus."

Though no one else was as articulate as Dave, the majority shared the same sentiment. Dale arrived at the conclusion that, depending on the circumstances, allowing abortion is a more compassionate choice than not allowing it. Marcus also supported women having the right to choose to have an abortion. As did Steve, who explained that he is no longer pro-life because, from a biological standpoint, he no longer believes personhood begins at conception. For him, a fetus becomes a person with rights when it becomes sentient. Shelley, who had an abortion when she was younger, admitted that she would do it again under the same circumstances. She would not feel as bad doing it today, as an atheist, than she did when she was a believer. The reason is that she now believes she has better information about the nature of what it means to be a human. Previously, she based her beliefs on religious convictions, whereas now, she bases her beliefs on her understanding of science.

Sexual Ethics

The issue of homosexuality and same-sex marriage was one that my conversation partners felt passionately about. They all accepted homosexuality as an alternative lifestyle and also supported same-sex marriage. Both of these positions are contrary to the traditional Christian understanding of marriage and sexuality. Interestingly, not all participants originally accepted the traditional Christian interpretations. Mitch and Anne both agreed that for them, homosexuality was something they never had any problems with when they were Christians. For those, unlike Mitch and Anne, who did adopt the traditional Christian interpretation on homosexuality, they jettisoned it when they deconverted.

Douglas admitted that, prior to his deconversion, he was adamantly against homosexuality. After his faith exit, homosexuality is a lifestyle that he has no problem with and a social cause that he supports to a great degree. When he was a Christian, embracing LGBTQ rights would have caused a major rift between him and his Christian community. Today, fighting for LGBTQ rights is something he is in favor of and engages in. Donald realized that once he no longer looked to the Bible as a guide to moral issues, homosexuality was something that he could no longer label as wrong. He freely admitted that he personally finds homosexuality unappealing, but that was insufficient grounds to condemn it:

> I don't think I have any grounds to call it wrong, like really wrong anymore, but I would be lying if I said that I am perfectly comfortable with that. It's not my thing, you know, but it is also something that I need to remind myself that I have really no grounds to think that it's wrong.

Frank's change of perspective was immediate. He realized that when biblical teachings no longer served as the foundation of his morality, he had no grounds to condemn homosexuality. One reason he had such a visceral reaction to becoming an advocate for LGBTQ rights was that the church, in his opinion, had not gotten as upset over divorce. On the one hand, this bothered him because Frank believed that Jesus was clear on the evils of divorce, but the church seems to tolerate it. And on the other hand, Jesus was silent on homosexuality, but the church never ceases to speak of its evils. The inconsistency and hypocrisy of that bothered him greatly.

Rachel acknowledged that she still didn't know whether gays and lesbians were born that way, if they choose to be gay, or a combination of the two. Nevertheless, she is inclined to believe that whatever orientation an individual has, they have the right to be happy and the right to be who they choose to be. For these reasons, she is now in favor of gay marriage. Cindy, post-Christianity, came to believe that gays and lesbians should be able to get married. Her rationale was that practicing gays and lesbians weren't hurting her or anyone else. Therefore, she felt that she had no basis to say that what they were doing was wrong. Finally, Wayne pointed to sexuality as the area that, for him, changed the most as a result of his deconversion. He not only changed his views on homosexuality; he also changed his views on every area of sexuality, now believing that virtually every kind of previously prohibited sexual behavior was acceptable:

> I would say the biggest area it has affected me has been sexuality . . . certain things like pornography or sex before marriage or like homosexuality. All these things I used to think . . . are wrong. I don't have to think they are wrong anymore. I had to completely reanalyze what it is that makes a thing like that right or wrong.

Intellectual Improvements

The individuals who shared their stories with me felt not only ethically freer but also intellectually freer after their deconversions. In some cases, deconversion resulted from their beliefs changing, and in others, the criteria for belief changed as a result of their deconversion. For example, those who deconverted because of intellectual problems shifted their criteria for truth, at some point, from the Bible to something else, typically reason or science. In other cases, the criteria for belief changed only after deconversion had taken place, and the Bible was no longer a viable option. In either case, they described the intellectual impacts of deconversion in positive terms. First, they felt freer in the sense that they were more open-minded. Second, they now based their beliefs on evidence, not faith. Third, science, not the Bible, had become their criterion of truth.

Openness

Charlene expressed her freedom to search for answers outside the Bible by arguing, "There is so much we don't know and so much we will never know, but rather than confining things into a small box [the Bible], I want to explore and search and learn more."

Marcus reported a similar attitude concerning the search for truth. "I feel like whatever the truth may be in all of this, I guess, I'm happy that I'm doing my best to discover what the truth is like about existence and stuff like that."

Steve was careful that, upon his deconversion, he did not immediately give up one belief system for another one. Instead, he took his time and investigated the issues. He realized how easy it is to get into what he called "groupthink." "I wanted my thoughts to be my thoughts, and I didn't want the group mentality to kind of dictate what I thought or believed," he said.

Basing Beliefs on Evidence

Faith in God is considered a virtue for Christians. Without trusting in the existence of God, one cannot meet the most basic criterion for being a Christian. Former Christians had, at one time in their lives, faith in God, but then lost it for various reasons. The loss of faith in God also resulted in a loss of faith in faith itself as a means of knowledge. Whereas before they looked to their faith tradition to discern true beliefs from false ones, they no longer did so after their deconversions. However, because it's difficult to live without an ultimate criterion for truth, they turned to empirical evidence.

Christopher now bases his beliefs only on strong empirical evidence. As an example, he shared an anecdote about when he was presented with a claim for a particular medical treatment that he thought to be questionable. He argued with the young woman about the legitimacy of the treatment but admitted that, despite how ridiculous it sounded to him, if she showed him research, he would look at it. If she could produce a study published in a recognized scholarly scientific journal in favor of the treatment, he would admit he was wrong and apologize. She didn't provide him with the evidence he required, so he withheld belief in the treatment.

Not accepting truth claims without substantial empirical evidence was also true of Charlene and Mitch. They both had come to the place where they no longer believed that biblical reasons were sufficient for any important belief they might hold. Each needed what they considered to be better reasons than the Bible commanding an action or making a truth claim if they were going to act on or believe the claim. One of the most common claims made by former believers as it relates to the cognitive nature of their new belief system is that the strength of one's beliefs should be proportional to the evidence. This was of particular importance to Mitch. Quoting Christopher Hitchens, he said, "Extraordinary claims require extraordinary evidence," by which he meant that if he was ever to accept something so extraordinary such as the resurrection of Jesus from the dead, he would need extraordinary evidence for it. But he was convinced that such evidence did not exist. Therefore, it would be wrong for him to believe in the resurrection. He considered this to be a more scientific mindset that was based on evidence, not faith. He speculated that this was the case not only for him but for other atheists as well. "So, I think you'll find that, when you talk to a lot of atheists, they tend to value things based on evidence, that evidence is the best way to explain things for now," he said. "I think that's a good way to live your life."

Tim concurred with Mitch's assessment of the importance evidence should play in forming beliefs. For Tim, the bottom line was, "Can you prove it?" He recounted a discussion with an individual over the truthfulness of the Bible that highlighted the role that evidence played for him in belief formation:

I say, "Can you back this up with evidence that doesn't come from the Bible?" Before long, he says "Verse . . ." and I was like, "No, no, no, I want evidence," and that's how I approach everything. So, that's how I approach it. Everything is evidence-based. If you can prove it, if it can be confirmed, if multiple people, multiple sources can confirm this, then, alright, I'm on board. . . . That's just how I approach every-thing; I'm very evidence-based.

Science

The evidence that former Christians were looking for was empirical, scientific evidence. They were not so much interested in philosophi-cal arguments or personal experience, but scientific facts. Anne cited science as her ultimate criterion for truth because it started giving her answers to her questions of ultimate concern. Being more passionate about science than she was about atheism, she claimed, "I wouldn't say I became more atheist. I became more science-oriented. I'm more into science than in the idea of atheism." She added, "I'm huge on you should only believe in what you actually test." After deconverting, Dale poured himself into various scientific disciplines in search of answers as well. He read a lot of books about physics, neuroscience, and biol-ogy in search of answers. The answers he discovered were much more meaningful and intriguing to him than the answers he received from the Bible.

At one time, Jill's ultimate criterion for determining the truth was the Bible but, like so many others, she now looks to science as her only authority. She places great weight on what she refers to as the scientific method. However, she did not explain just what she thought that was. When asked what she believed was the best means of testing knowledge claims, Rachel also pointed to science. "I'm probably more scientific about things, and I see things more scientifically, more than spiritually." What attracted her to science over other approaches was that science is constantly changing and is based on empirical evidence:

What I like about science is that [scientists] are constantly learning; they are constantly studying, you know. And, I really like the fact of science being able to, I guess, guide me a little bit. Not because it's one hundred percent true, but I think I like the discovery; I like the learning. I like the discovery, I guess, the reason and, you know, evidenced-based, for sure.

After deconverting, Wayne returned to one of the early loves in his life. He claimed, "I definitely fell in love with science again." As a child, he grew up watching space-related television shows and recalled how he was into space exploration. He's optimistic that, as humans, we are becoming good skeptics who don't just take the word of religious authorities as the ultimate criterion of truth. Rather than looking to faith, Wayne said he, like Jill, was looking to the scientific method to guide him into the truth about the world he lives in.

Worth the Cost

Like Olga, the holocaust survivor I met while washing windows, deconverts feel liberated from their captors. In the case of Olga, it was the Nazis; in the case of former Christians, it was the Christian religion. They consistently reported that they are better off emotionally, ethically, and intellectually. Emotionally, this means they are happier than when they were Christians, due to losing negative characteristics and gaining positive ones. Ethically, they feel they have improved by becoming more compassionate and tolerant of others. Intellectually, they are now free to think for themselves, which translates into the belief that they are on more secure footing concerning the rationality of their beliefs. Science and reason became the criteria they utilize in determining what is worth believing.

That former believers both believe and feel that they are emotionally, ethically, and intellectually better off after they left Christianity is interesting, in and of itself. But what is more significant is that, despite the numerous negative results they incurred when they left their faith, deconverts repeatedly testify that it was all worth it for the freedom they obtained. This raises many questions about just what kind of Christianity they deconverted from and if it contributed to their loss of faith. In the next and final section, I will offer several suggestions on how to avoid setting up believers for a loss of faith and also how to provide them with a solid foundation upon which to build a faith that endures.

PART 3

APPLICATION

CHAPTER ELEVEN

AVOIDING AND AVERTING

Setting the Table

In this chapter, I will do three things. First, I will briefly recap what we have discovered. Second, I will offer practical advice on how we can avoid setting up believers for a loss of faith or a serious crisis of faith (this is applicable to those who believe in eternal security and to those who don't). My advice will focus on helping believers have a flexible faith that can endure intellectual challenges and will equip them well for our current cultural climate. This consists of evaluating what kind of faith we are passing on to believers. Are we overburdening believers with having to believe nonessential doctrines in order to be a "real" or "biblical" Christian? If so, we need to reconsider doing that. Third, I will look at how we can avert a loss of faith for a Christian who is struggling to believe. I will do so by seeking to undermine some of the unspoken and perhaps unconscious assumptions that many deconverts hold. The idea here is to defuse the objection not by providing an answer but instead by diminishing the force of the objection by demonstrating that the assumptions that underwrite it are unjustified.

Discoveries

I trust that the discoveries of this study are meaningful for the church. I hope that Christians will find the study meaningful because it provides them with insights as to how they are viewed by those who once identified with them. We can all benefit from hearing how others view us. And, although it might be hard to hear, if there is truth in their perceptions, we will be better for listening to it. I imagine it is shocking to hear that many who deconvert do so for the reason that their experience as a Christian was so negative that the best way to describe leaving the faith was liberation and a significant improvement in their well-being. And yet, if that is the case, we need to ask why. What kind of Christianity did they experience that caused them to feel burdened and weighed down to such an extent that deconverting was analogous to having a weight lifted off their shoulders? Why do they feel that they are morally and intellectually in a better place after their faith exit as opposed to when they were Christians? These questions, in and of themselves, are interesting, but they take on a sense of urgency when combined with certain facts. What does it say about the kind of Christianity that they were socialized into when, despite losing some of the most important relationships in their lives, deconverts said it was worth it for the freedom they found? Think about that for a minute.

We are, above nearly all else, social creatures created to live in community with one another. One of the most severe punishments we hand out to criminals is solitary confinement. Why? Because even above our freedom, we need and value interaction with others. Given the choice between living on an island alone for the rest of one's life and being incarcerated with others, I suspect most of us would choose the latter. What does that say, then, about the Christian experience that deconverts had, given that, despite the fact that it might mean they would lose some of the most meaningful and life-giving relationships if they were to leave the faith, they did so anyway?

A further benefit of the study, I trust, is that it raises the importance of seeking answers to the vexing questions that surround faith exits— questions such as: Why was it that deconverts found their Christian environments morally and cognitively inferior to what they discovered in their life after faith? It would be tempting to lay all the blame on the deconverted by claiming that they experienced discipleship as existentially burdensome and intellectually and morally backwards because they were hard-hearted and unwilling to submit to the claims of Christ. I'm sure that is the case for some of them. But I'm convinced that many deconverts experienced a sense of freedom and intellectual and moral advance after leaving the faith because the Christian environments they were socialized in were sources of intellectual discouragement and moral lethargy. They had become legalistic, prideful, and self-righteous, and, in their desire to remain "biblical," they had forgotten that the Sabbath had been made for man, not the other way around. By that, I simply mean that their interpretation of the Bible and the system of truth that they had come to naively identify with pure, unadorned Christianity itself had become more important to uphold and demand allegiance to than the reason why the Bible had been given in the first place, which is that individuals could learn of the story of God and his desire to have a relationship with them. Part of what that means is believing the truth as it is laid out in Scripture. I'm not saying that having positions on issues and doctrines is unimportant. But, like the Pharisees, who were so focused on the law that they crucified the very one who gave the law, churches and parents can become so focused on their particular understanding of the Bible and what it means to be a genuine Christian that they can forget the purpose of the Bible and, as a result, drive away individuals from the faith by how they use the Bible.

This study raises important questions not only for the church but also for those who have left the faith. It does so by revealing not just the general contours of the impact of deconversion, but it also brings to light important presuppositions that many deconverts hold but might not be aware of. Recognizing these can prove advantageous to Christians who are in dialogue with those who are wrestling with their faith. By knowing the presuppositions that often underwrite faith loss, parents and church leaders can hopefully address the deeper causal factors that lie beneath the surface but that wield incredible power when it comes to deconversion.

Avoiding

As Christians, we would do well to consider the results of this study for the sake of those we minister to. The fact that the participants of both this study and others report that they feel liberated as a result of leaving the Christian faith should be deeply troubling. We should also be concerned that former Christians believe they discovered the real truth about the Bible from sources outside the church. These findings raise two questions we would do well to ponder. The first is, how can we avoid passing on a system of belief that is faithful to the historic Christian faith without it being experienced as a weight around a believer's neck? The second is, how can we avoid believers being deeply troubled to the point of having a crisis of belief by what they discover about the nature, history, and composition of the Bible? The answer to the first question, it seems to me, is that we avoid instilling a stifling and restrictive faith in believers by placing on them no greater burden than necessary for them to be Christians. The answer to the second question is to inoculate them against having such a crisis by exposing them to the history, nature, and composition of the Bible in a safe environment, one that is not afraid to honestly recognize that the Bible, while being a divine book, is also a very human book. Sometimes that means it will not look the way we might expect it to upon closer examination, but that is okay.

No Greater Burden

In the book of Acts, the early church found itself on the verge of a split. Certain Jewish Christians in the church at Antioch were forcefully arguing that in order for gentile converts to be saved, they must not only believe in Jesus but also obey Mosaic law, specifically the rite of circumcision. As one would guess, the gentile converts were not as enthusiastic about that idea as the Judaizers were. Paul and Barnabas sided with the gentiles, arguing that salvation was not dependent on keeping the law but on faith in Christ. To settle the issue, the disputants agreed to take the issue to the apostles and elders in Jerusalem and let them decide the matter.

Ultimately, the apostles sided with Paul and Barnabas and agreed that the gentiles did not need to be circumcised or keep the law of Moses in order to be saved. After the decision was made, the apostles and elders wrote the leadership at Antioch the following letter:

To the Gentile believers in Antioch, Syria and Cilicia:

Greetings.
We have heard that some went out from us without our authorization and disturbed you, troubling your minds by what they said. So we all agreed to choose some men and send them to you with our dear friends Barnabas and Paul—men who have risked their lives for the name of our Lord Jesus Christ. Therefore we are sending Judas and Silas to confirm by word of mouth what we are writing. It seemed good to the Holy Spirit and to us not to burden you with anything beyond the following requirements: You are to abstain from food sacrificed to idols, from blood, from the meat of strangled animals and from sexual immorality. You will do well to avoid these things. (Acts 15:23–29)

The phrase that I want to focus on in the above passage is: "It seemed good to the Holy Spirit and to us not to burden you with anything beyond the following requirements." Why did they conclude that it was important to avoid placing an unnecessary burden on the gentile believers? I suspect it's because the apostles wisely recognized the damage that would be done by requiring the gentiles to adopt practices and beliefs that were not essential to the faith. They discerned that the faith of the gentile believers might buckle under the weight of numerous or onerous nonessential requirements. Allowing the Jewish believers in Antioch to place upon the gentile believers a list of beliefs and practices they needed to perform in order to be Christians would ultimately drive them away from the faith or split the church into a Jewish faction and a gentile faction. Therefore, since it was not necessary for being saved, they instructed the church at Antioch that the gentiles did not need to keep the Mosaic law. In doing so, they, no doubt, prevented gentile believers from leaving the faith. There is a lesson here for parents and church leaders.

Stories of those who have left the faith are frequently set in church contexts that burdened believers with the obligation to affirm every belief and practice of that particular church in order to be a Christian. As in Antioch, certain Christian communities have an interpretation of what is essential to believe in order to be a Christian that goes well beyond what is necessary. It's true that there are essential Christian doctrines that need to be believed in order to experience true spiritual transformation, and still other beliefs that cannot be denied if one wants to be within the bounds of historic Christian orthodoxy. The problem comes, however, when communities construct their beliefs in such a way that the structure depends on all the beliefs in such a way that if one belief is rejected, the entire edifice will collapse. Recently, I read an account of Daniel Wallace, director of the Center for the Study of New Testament Manuscripts, where he shared how his faith, at one time, was constructed in such an all-or-nothing fashion. While on Christmas break from his studies at seminary, Wallace returned home and met with his uncle, a Christian scholar from a different theological tradition than the conservative evangelical world he inhabited. In order to find out just what his uncle believed, he decided to engage him in some doctrinal Q&A:

> I came home to California for a Christmas vacation early on in the program. And I had lunch with my uncle, David Wallace. He was the first graduate from Fuller Seminary to earn a PhD. He earned it at Edinburgh University, under Matthew Black. But he also logged some time in various places in Europe—studying with Baumgartner, Barth, and others. He was not pleased with my choice to attend Dallas Seminary; I was clueless about what he really believed. During the lunch, I asked him what he thought about inerrancy. His response startled me and changed my perspective

for all time. He essentially said that he didn't hold to the doctrine (though he said so much more colorfully than that!). I thought to myself, "Oh no! My uncle is going to hell!"[1]

Why would Wallace think that his uncle would go to hell because he did not affirm inerrancy? The answer is simple. For Wallace, Christianity was a packaged deal of all-or-nothing beliefs that included the doctrine of inerrancy. Therefore, if someone didn't affirm inerrancy, they were not a Christian. At some point in his past, Wallace was either explicitly taught or had implicitly caught the idea that inerrancy is an essential doctrine to uphold in order to be a Christian. Naturally, then, he was concerned when his uncle did not affirm it. In Wallace's understanding, believing in inerrancy was just as important to be a Christian as believing in the resurrection. I suspect that if he were asked at the time if that were the case, he would have said no. But the doctrine of inerrancy had risen so high in his echelon of beliefs that, for all practical purposes, it had become an essential doctrine. There are any number of doctrines that can be elevated to the status of an essential belief in an all-or-nothing approach to faith. For churches that subscribe to such an approach, the set of doctrines that make up the sum total of beliefs one needs to affirm in order to be a Christian is different. But what they all have in common is an all-or-nothing package of beliefs that need to be affirmed in total in order to be a Christian.

Fred Clark, the former managing editor of *Prism* magazine, says that although from the outside, all-or-nothing faith doesn't seem to make much sense, this is because the separate components of the package do seem separable. He says, "From the outside, it just seems kind of silly to insist that, for example, belief in the Golden Rule requires and is somehow dependent on belief that the universe is only 6,000 years old."[2] He goes on to say that from the inside, however, things look a lot different:

---

[1] Daniel Wallace, "My Take on Inerrancy," Bible.org, August 10, 2006.
[2] Fred Clark, "The All-or-Nothing Lie of Fundamentalist Christianity (Part 1)," *The Slacktivist* (blog), December 3, 2012.

Belief in Jesus, in forgiveness, or in faith, hope and love, really does come to seem contingent and dependent upon all those other beliefs in inerrancy, literalism, creationism, and whichever weird American variant of eschatology your particular sub-group of fundies subscribes to. And that means, for those shaped by fundamentalism, that belief in Jesus, faith, hope and love are all constantly imperiled by even fleeting glimpses of reality. Some such glimpse will eventually penetrate the protective fundie shell—the recognition that maybe all sedimentary rocks didn't come from Noah's flood, the realization that the Synoptic Gospels can't be easily "harmonized," the attempt to evangelize some Hell bound Episcopalian that results in them getting the better of the conversation. And when that happens, the whole edifice threatens to topple like some late-in-the-game Jenga tower.[3]

The problem does not end with requiring an all-or-nothing system of faith in which every belief depends on every other belief. That would be bad enough. It gets compounded when the package that must be accepted is identified as something called "biblical Christianity." Such adjectives give the impression that there is one correct way to be a Christian, the biblical way, and that all others are substandard. And that one way is identical to the all-or-nothing package of a particular church. In reality, however, what is assumed to be "biblical Christianity" is an admixture of core theological truths and the micro-traditions and particular interpretations of one particular church or denomination. What this all-or-nothing misidentification results in is the demand that, in order to be a Christian, one must affirm and adopt an entire set of beliefs and practices, without exception, that contain many traditions and convictions that are not necessary in order to be a Christian.

Identifying "biblical" Christianity with one's own church or denomination this way is highly problematic. First, it ignores the indisputable fact that, throughout history, there have been an enormous number

---

[3] Clark, "All-or-Nothing Lie."

of Christian traditions that stand well within orthodoxy but that look very different from each other in secondary and tertiary beliefs, as well as practices. Admittedly, it is true that all of them could be in error in how they interpret and apply the Bible, and that one tradition—the tradition of the pre-deconvert—is the only tradition throughout the history of the church that is the truly biblical version. However, this line of thinking strains credulity to the point of breaking. And yet, that is exactly what the all-or-nothing package version of the faith implies, if not entails. Burdening individuals with a requirement that, in order to be a Christian, they must believe all the various doctrines of one particular church is to place on them a weight too heavy to bear and one that will, in all likelihood, set them up for a crisis of faith.

The second problem with requiring believers to adopt a large, inflexible, and fragile set of beliefs and practices is that it makes the Christian life tedious and joyless and tends to make people negative and critical. As we have seen, former believers look back on their time in the church with regret and, in some cases, shame at how they viewed others. Because their Christian system gave them the impression that they were "biblical" believers because they adhered to the correct form of Christianity, they became self-righteous and critical. At the same time, they buckled under the weight of having to continually find ways to justify beliefs that had become harder and harder to believe, given information about the world they were becoming convinced of. On top of that, they could no longer maintain the standards of conduct that were expected of them by their Christian community. For many, the level of commitment expected by their churches was so high that it strained relationships with family, friends, and employers, and it sometimes even put a burden on their finances. Like the Pharisees, who Jesus accused of binding heavy burdens on the shoulders of men but who themselves would not lift a finger to help, such churches place equally heavy burdens on Christians and set them up to develop resentment toward Christianity. Who would want to be part of a group that demands so much and, in return, produces beat-down, critical people?

I trust that by now the application for us is obvious. Christians of all stripes must reflect on the kind of faith they are passing on to those they are ministering to. Is it a fragile and bloated house of cards comprising core tenets of the faith and our own micro-traditions elevated to the level of orthodoxy that must be believed in order to be saved? Or is it stable, secure, and built on a solid foundation? An overly strict home or church life that imposes unbiblical rules upon believers acts only to push individuals toward apostasy rather than keep them from it. The irony is that the very means by which some churches have used to keep their people within the fold significantly contributed to their deconversions. There is clearly something wrong with an interpretation of Christianity that places heavy burdens on believers when Jesus says that his burden is light and his truth is freeing. This raises the question of just what deconverts are rejecting. It certainly is not the religion of Jesus of Nazareth.

I suspect that some may be thinking that the real problem lies in the fact that some deconverts simply did not want to submit to the kingship of Jesus and that, regardless of how healthy their home or church environment was, they would bristle at being told anything that required them to surrender any amount of autonomy. There is no doubt that the gospel is a call to recognize the kingship of Jesus and submit to his reign and rule in one's life. This means that we must relinquish control of our lives and live in accordance with his will. Sometimes, perhaps many times, his will goes against the grain of our own sinful inclinations. We all will feel the temptation to usurp his authority in our lives and live according to our own desires. Following Jesus can, at times, feel burdensome, frustrating, and as though our freedom has been curtailed. In return, however, Jesus promises to provide us with an abundant life, true joy, and a path toward being the kind of humans we were created to be. In short, Jesus promises us that if we make him king, he will make us flourish. In the case of untold numbers of deconverts, that was not the case. They did not experience the abundant life, joy, and flourishing that Jesus offers because the Christian environments they were formed in applied so many extra requirements for them to believe or perform that the joy of Jesus was snuffed out by the demands of a religious system. There is no getting away from this fact.

Immune to Criticism

Immunization is a controversial subject today. Despite the fact that we now possess the ability to prevent children from contracting deadly diseases via immunization, some parents, out of an abundance of caution, refuse to have their children immunized. Why is that? Parents who choose to have their children not receive vaccinations believe that the risks outweigh the benefits. And what are those risks? That the children will contract either the disease they are being inoculated against, or that they will develop another condition resulting from the combination of vaccines. The vast majority of parents, however, believe the benefits outweigh the risks. Because of immunization, children today are no longer in danger of suffering and dying from an array of diseases that children only a few generations ago were. In terms of life-changing medical discoveries, vaccinations rank near the top of the list. In 1796, Edward Jenner vaccinated a thirteen-year-old boy with cowpox, resulting in him becoming immune to smallpox. Two years later, a smallpox vaccine was created, and within two hundred years, smallpox was eradicated. Cholera, diphtheria, and polio vaccines followed. The effectiveness of vaccinations in protecting children from some of the worst kinds of diseases cannot be overstated, which raises the question of how vaccines work. What Jenner and others discovered is that children become immune to diseases like measles, mumps, smallpox, and rubella by being exposed to them in small dosages. Exposure to these diseases in the form of their antigens—the non-dangerous element of the disease—in a controlled manner creates in the bodies of children antibodies that make them immune to ever contracting the disease in its deadly form. I am advocating something similar in terms of preventing believers from contracting a fatal crisis of faith.

In order to protect believers from the most common challenges that lead to a crisis of faith, they need to be inoculated against such challenges. This is done by ensuring that believers are initially exposed to challenges in a safe environment by knowledgeable Christians. Given that the most common and effective objections to the Christian faith revolve around the Bible, it is these issues that deserve our attention. Believers should be exposed to Old Testament "terror texts," the problems raised by historical criticism, and various textual discrepancies of the Bible by other believers before they are acquainted with them by unbelievers. By doing so, many potential problems can be avoided. Just knowing that Christians are aware of the challenges and have responded to many of them is sometimes all that is needed to defuse a prospective crisis of faith. On the contrary, however, finding out about many of the challenges that are brought against the Bible from unbelievers can be devastating. Not a few former believers report that they felt deceived and even lied to by fellow Christians when they discovered the backstory of the Bible in terms of its composition and content. And make no mistake, more and more believers will be exposed to this information by skeptics and anti-theistic apologists via the Internet. Christians, especially those of high school and college ages, need to be exposed to the troubling elements of the text of Scripture from a Christian perspective before they encounter those problems from critical, skeptical sources. Issues such as historical discrepancies, authorship of texts, errors in transmission, inclusion of inauthentic passages (such as the long ending of Mark), and the process of canonization need to be raised by Christian leaders.

Furthermore, believers need to be inoculated against the false dilemma of having to affirm nonessential doctrines or renounce their faith. This is done by refusing to draw hard lines on issues such as the inerrancy of Scripture or the incompatibility of evolution with the existence of God. Doing so has proven to be a catalyst in the deconversion process. Clear thinking on these issues should result in a reevaluation of both positions. Logically, there is no contradiction in holding that Christianity is true and that evolution is the means by which God created humans. Admittedly, this will demand reading certain texts of Scripture from a different perspective. But a different perspective does not necessarily entail an unbiblical one. Additionally, conservatives must not make inerrancy a criterion for being a true believer. Perhaps even more problematic is the claim often made by Christians that if there is one error in the Bible, it cannot be the Word of God. What is tragic about this claim is that it forces reflective believers who have encountered serious challenges to the doctrine of inerrancy to depend entirely on the discipline of apologetics to retain their faith. The fact that numerous volumes have been written attempting to demonstrate the inerrancy of the Bible is evidence, in and of itself, that the claim "If the Bible has even one error, it is not the Word of God" sets believers up for apostasy. With so many alleged errors to choose from, is it really reasonable to think that apologists can refute all of them to such a degree that all reasonable people will find the answers acceptable? For many former believers, because inerrancy was elevated to the level of an essential truth, losing belief in that doctrine was analogous to pulling a card out of a house of cards. And, like any house of cards does when a card gets pulled out, their faith fell flat as a pancake.

Lest you think I am bashing the doctrine of inerrancy, let me make it clear—I am not. I affirm inerrancy. The problem is not with the doctrine that the Bible is without error. Instead, the problem is twofold. The first is when the entire edifice of the faith is either implicitly or explicitly made to rest on the Bible having to be inerrant. The second is requiring individuals to affirm that the Bible is inerrant in order to be genuine believers. Concerning the first problem, it should be obvious that, from a historical point of view, the Bible does not have to be inerrant in order to ground our faith; it just needs to be reliable enough that we can have confidence that what it tells us about the life, death, and resurrection of Jesus is true. The argument that if there is one error in the Bible that we cannot trust what it teaches at any point is categorically false and does not logically follow. Concerning the second problem, I hope that a bit of reflection will also make it clear that in order to be a genuine Christian, one does not have to affirm inerrancy.

The Bible's claim for itself is that it is inspired. It nowhere states that it is inerrant. I am not denying that both a logical/theological and a scriptural argument can be made supporting the conclusion that the

Bible is inerrant. But that is a different matter than the Bible explicitly stating that it's inerrant. God-honoring, Scripture-loving Christians throughout history have held different positions on the inerrancy of the Bible. So, while affirming the inerrancy of the Bible may be the practice of a particular Christian denomination, church, or even family teaching, it's wrong to imply or explicitly claim that in order to be a real Christian, one must believe in inerrancy. Doing so adds a burden to their faith that is not necessary for them to carry. If inerrancy is a doctrine that one wants to pass on to those who they are discipling, then they must teach it accurately. This means explaining what is and is not considered an error, according to the doctrine. Far too many former believers exhibit a distorted understanding of the doctrine of inerrancy, which sets them up for a crisis. Assuming that inerrancy means applying a strict and overly literal view of truth to the Bible, they found what they considered errors in the text. However, had they been educated about what inerrancy actually is, they would have found far fewer examples of errors.

Given the fact that so many former believers point to problems with the Bible being the catalyst for their deconversions, it is imperative that church leaders and parents be the first to expose their children and those to whom they minister to the challenges raised above. It also means that inerrancy, while an important secondary doctrine, should not be elevated to the level of a nonnegotiable that the faith rests upon. When inerrancy is taught, it must be done accurately in order to avoid instilling in believers an expectation that the Bible will not live up to.

Averting

In order to assist those who are wrestling with their faith and contemplating whether or not they can continue to identify as believers, it's important to have a handle on what may be driving their doubts. There are always certain presuppositions, the vast majority of which are held unconsciously, that give doubts their force. If addressed successfully, the doubt will lose its force, if not evaporate entirely. As mentioned above, the unquestioned presupposition that the Bible must be inerrant or that Genesis must be read literally are common among former

Christians. Believing that they must accept both doctrines in order to be a genuine Christian, former believers lost their faith when they lost the ability to force themselves to believe in either teaching. Another assumption that is evident in the stories of nearly all former Christians is that they are thoroughgoing evidentialists.

Evidentialism

Evidentialism is characterized by the dictum that it's only rational to believe that for which there is adequate evidence. Evidence, in this case, is understood to be arguments that are grounded in self-evident truths or empirical, scientific data. In the case of those I interacted with, before their deconversions, a quarter of them looked to apologetics in order to undergird their faith. The apologetics in question were typically evidentialist in nature and placed a great deal of weight on being able to use both philosophical arguments and empirical data to demonstrate the truthfulness of Christianity. When deconverts encountered objections they couldn't refute, their evidentialist presuppositions forced them to conclude that Christianity was either false or that committing oneself to it was rationally unjustifiable, given the lack of evidence. It appears that it never occurred to them that another option was available, which was to doubt their evidentialist presupposition as the criterion of rationality, yet there is good reason to do so.

Evidentialism as the sole criterion for the rationality of belief has been critiqued as far back as 1896. William James, in his seminal lecture titled "The Will to Believe," attacked the strident evidentialism that held many epistemically captive in his day. More recently, Alvin Plantinga,[4] Nicholas Wolterstorff,[5] George Mavrodes,[6] and William Alston[7] have

---

[4] Alvin Planting, *Warranted Christian Belief* (Oxford: Oxford University Press, 2000).

[5] Nicholas Wolterstorff, *Faith and Rationality: Reason and Belief in God* (Notre Dame, IN: University of Notre Dame Press, 1984).

[6] George Mavrodes, *Belief in God: A Study in the Epistemology of Religion* (New York: Random House, 1970).

[7] William Alston, *Perceiving God: The Epistemology of Religious Experience* (Ithaca, NY: Cornell University Press, 1993).

offered powerful critiques of evidentialism in relation to the rationality of belief in the existence of God. They have all argued that evidentialism is irrelevant when it comes to determining if belief in the existence of God is rational. They do so by persuasively demonstrating that evidentialism is impotent to justify the belief in the existence of other minds. Yet, we are rational in believing in the existence of minds other than our own. If that is true, they argue, then we should also be rational in believing in the existence of God without meeting the strict requirements of evidentialism because God essentially is a mind, soul, or center of consciousness. Those who agree with the above philosophers point out that not only is evidentialism irrelevant to whether our belief in other minds is rational; it is also slightly obstinate. Does it not seem perverse to demand the kind of evidence that evidentialism requires before we are willing to allow that our family and friends are conscious agents, not automatons? Raising this critique with those who place a great deal of weight on empirical evidence to determine whether or not they will believe in God may be helpful because it forces them to justify a foundational assumption that they likely have never realized they hold. In doing so, they may realize that their objection rests on a faulty foundation, one that does not support the conclusion that in order to rationally believe in God, one must have empirical evidence.

Furthermore, a new, more solid foundation for belief in God can replace a faulty evidentialist foundation. For example, if an individual is troubled by the fact that they find none of the evidential arguments for God's existence persuasive, they may still be able to rationally maintain their belief in God based on other factors. Instead of concluding that the belief that God exists must be supported by a long chain of objective evidence ending in some sort of self-evident belief, they may recognize that it is eminently rational to take the claim that God exists as a properly basic belief grounded in immediate experience alone. While this approach to thinking about the existence of God may not be palatable for those committed to evidentialism, it may provide a means by which those who are committed to holding rationally justified beliefs to maintain belief in God. At the very least, critiquing evidentialism and offering a more holistic approach to justifying beliefs may open the eyes of skeptical believers to the fact that they possess many assumptions that impact their surface-level beliefs. Hopefully, by becoming aware of that fact, skeptical believers will be inclined toward greater intellectual humility in evaluating the evidence and restraint in abandoning their Christian commitment.

Scientism

Consistent with their evidentialist epistemology, deconverts demonstrated a great appreciation for science as the primary source for acquiring knowledge. This appreciation bordered on scientism. Scientism is the belief that science, and science alone, can provide objective knowledge about reality. This is a naive view of science and betrays a lack of understanding about the foundation upon which all knowledge claims are built. Deconverts would benefit from investigating the philosophical underpinnings of science. While science has proven to be a remarkably successful discipline, it is not the paradigm of objectivity that many believe it is.

First, all scientific observations are theory-laden, which means they are not unadulterated, presuppositionless apprehensions of brute facts about reality. All facts are interpreted through a host of assumptions that often operate at the subconscious level and never achieve complete epistemic objectivity.

Second, scientific theories that attempt to provide explanations for states of affairs are always underdetermined by the data and, thus, are never certain. In order for a theory to be considered successful in explaining a state of affairs, it must fall within the limits of what is considered an acceptable range of deviation. However, different fields of science allow for differing ranges. What is within an acceptable range of deviation for spectroscopy is not within the acceptable range for stellar magnitude. So, whether a theory successfully accounts for a particular state of affairs depends on what field it is. There is no uniform agreement across the various scientific disciplines on what constitutes an acceptable range of deviation.

Third, it's a common misunderstanding that what makes science an objective discipline, as opposed to philosophy or theology, is that science has a particular method that is at the heart of scientific investigation. It's true that many scientific experiments do utilize an inductive method, but there is no such thing as the one and only scientific method. There are a number of ways in which scientists approach their disciplines. For example, abduction, more commonly known as inference to arrive at the best explanation, seeks to discover which hypothesis best explains arrive at the total amount of data, given a certain set of facts. It requires a great deal of subjective judgment on the part of scientists, but it is, nonetheless, a common and acceptable scientific method.

Fourth, it's clearly the assumption of not only former Christians who point to science as the final arbiter of truth, but the general public as well, that what makes science special and worthy of our allegiance is that, through falsification and theory refinement, science is continually moving toward a more accurate understanding of reality. This is surely overstating the case. I am no science skeptic, but it does need to be pointed out that science "progresses" by way of funeral. By that, I mean science advances when theories that were once assumed to be correct are proven false and replaced by a new theory. There are two issues that need to be addressed in the above sentence. The first is the concept of "progress." As you can see, I have put that word in scare quotes to indicate that you should read it ironically. Why did I do that? The answer is that, although science has certainly allowed us to manage and manipulate the world to our own ends, it's not as clear that it has done so by discovering the truth about the nature of reality. Without going into details, there are good reasons to question whether what we believe about the world as revealed by science accurately reflects the way the world is, or whether science has merely discovered how to manipulate the world to meet our needs. That might sound shocking. Nevertheless, philosophers of science are divided on the issue. In looking at the history of science, it's clear that entire scientific paradigms that allowed us to control and manipulate the world to our own ends have been overthrown and replaced by other paradigms. What's most interesting about this is that the new paradigms are not merely readjustments of the previous paradigms but are entirely different paradigms governed by different assumptions. What this implies is that the previous paradigm, the one that was in place for years, if not centuries, and which was thought to be an accurate reflection of reality because it allowed us to make accurate predictions and control the physical world to meet our ends was wrong.

Thomas Kuhn has demonstrated this phenomenon of paradigm replacement throughout the history of science in his groundbreaking book *The Structure of Scientific Revolutions.*[8] Kuhn's work, along with the insights of other philosophers of science, has caused many to seriously consider adopting an anti-realist position regarding the claims of science. Anti-realists come in all stripes, but what they all have in common is that they believe, at least to some degree, that the claims of science are not true. By "true," I mean that some claims of science do not match up with reality. They may work, they may allow us to manipulate reality to our own ends via technology, but they do not accurately describe reality. As I said, anti-realists come in varying degrees. Some are radically skeptical that science is saying anything true about reality. Others are more optimistic and think that science is largely correct in its descriptions of the world but acknowledge that, in the past, we believed certain theories were true because of their success that today we take to be wrong. Perhaps theories we believe are true today because of their success will turn out to be false in the future. Regardless of where one lands on the realism/antirealism spectrum, it's important that those who point to science as a reason for their loss of faith or who now look to science as the final arbiter of what is rational are made aware of the limitations of science. More could be said about the limitations and assumptions of science, but suffice it to say, science is not the objective, unbiased means to knowledge that many take it to be. This is no criticism against science—it is merely intended to point out that deconverts have perhaps given too much credit where it is not due.

---

[8] Thomas Kuhn, *The Structure of Scientific Revolutions* (Chicago: University of Chicago Press, 1970).

Three Things

In this chapter, we have done three things. First, we looked back at the discoveries made by interviewing former believers about their journey from Christianity to some form of unbelief. We discovered that even though the price was high, all in all, it was worth paying for the sense of freedom that was experienced. Second, we looked at some of the ways we can avoid setting up individuals for a crisis of faith. It's important to point out that, whether or not one believes that a true Christian can lose their faith, the problems we focused on are ones that we should seek to avoid creating in the spiritual development of those whom we are entrusted to lead. Third, we identified the importance of averting spiritual disaster, or, as Paul would put it, "shipwreck" (1 Tim. 1:19), by exposing some of the expectations and assumptions that are motivators of faith crises. In the next chapter, we will investigate what we can do to cultivate and instill enduring faith in believers.

CHAPTER TWELVE

CULTIVATING FAITH

Sowing Seeds

In the parable of the sower (Matt. 13:1–23), Jesus tells the story of a farmer who went out to plant seeds. The farmer has varying degrees of success, depending on the kind of soil he planted his seeds in. Some seeds fell on the walking path but failed to take root because the ground was too hard and there was no way for the seeds to penetrate the soil. Other seeds fell on the rocky ground that lacked soil for the seeds to take root in. Still, other seeds fell among the thorns. Here, there was enough soil for the seeds to take root and grow, but they were ultimately choked out by the thorns and did not produce a harvest. Only the fourth soil, which Jesus refers to as the "good soil," took root and produced a crop for the farmer. Curious readers might wonder what it was about the good soil that made it "good." The Bible doesn't explicitly say, but there are only two possibilities. The first is that what made the good soil good was its composition. Some soil is just better for farming based on its makeup. Nutrient-rich soil that has beneficial organisms, good tilth, and sufficient depth is crucial to successful farming.[1] The second characteristic of good soil has less to do with the soil itself as it does the

---

[1] Lynn Kime, "Soil Quality Information," PennState Extension, August 28, 2012.

preparation of the soil. Good soil for planting crops not only has the characteristics just mentioned; it also has to be cultivated. Without preparing the soil to be able to receive the seeds, even the highest-quality soil won't yield the crop it's capable of. In the case of the parable of the sower, had the path where the seeds fell been tilled and broken up, perhaps the seeds would have taken root. If the rocky soil had been cleared of the rocks, then perhaps the seeds thrown on it would have taken root. And if the thorns had been cut out before the seeds were sown, they would have taken root and flourished. Cultivation of the soil is essential for seeds to have the best chance to take root and produce a harvest.

I take it that the personality traits, temperament, and personal values that individuals bring with them into their encounter with the Word of God are analogous to the makeup and composition of the soil. There is little we can do as parents and leaders to change those. What we can do, though, is prepare and cultivate the "soil" to give it the best chance of receiving the seed—the Word of God—when it's sown in their hearts. By doing so, we give it, humanly speaking, the best odds of going down deep into the hearts of the hearers, setting roots and producing fruit that is indicative of salvation. In the previous chapter, I looked at ways to remove some of the common impediments to producing faith. In this chapter, I will offer several suggestions on how to cultivate the soil that is the hearts of our children and those we minister to, so they are in a good position to hear and receive the Word.

The Limitations of Reason and the Necessity of Revelation

Whereas when they were believers, individuals looked to the Bible as their ultimate criterion of truth, in becoming unbelievers, deconverts exchanged the authority of the Bible for something they refer to as "reason" in order to determine what they would be willing to believe. What most do not recognize is that, in doing so, they have made two errors. First, they have mistaken reason for a thing—an ultimate authority or criterion—instead of a process or a tool. Second, they have not realized that the adoption of "reason" as their final authority is ultimately a presuppositional choice among other available options, and that all presuppositional choices are ultimately faith commitments. Their choice of "reason" is, to them, self-evident; but in reality, it is only one of several options one can choose from. It is crucial for believers to understand this.

Tool or standard? All reasoning is done according to an ultimate standard or authority that determines for an individual what claims they will accept as true. Everyone has a final arbiter of truth that they assume, whether they realize it or not. Most individuals simply assume that something they call "reason" is that final authority. It is crucial that we help believers see that reason is not, nor cannot be, one's final authority when it comes to judging truth claims because, first of all, it's not a "thing," but a process. It's a tool, not a standard.

Instead of holding that reason is an objective criterion for truth, we should help believers see that, in reality, it's a tool that humans have been endowed with from God in order to draw inferences and conclusions. A helpful way to think about reason is to see it as a process. We engage in reasoning, or we reason. It's an activity or an action, not primarily an object or thing. Our cognitive faculties act upon beliefs and opinions we already accept (often uncritically), which help us reach conclusions via what we see as inferences, implications, or entailments. If we are inclined to think of reason as a thing, a better way to think about it is as a tool. Perhaps the best way to illustrate this is to compare reason with a familiar tool such as a circular saw, which consists of a circular blade, an adjustable guide, a handle, and a trigger. The guide can be adjusted to various angles so when the trigger is pulled, the saw will cut according to the angle of the guide. Set the saw at a forty-five-degree angle, and it will produce a forty-five-degree cut. Set it at twenty-two degrees, and it will produce a twenty-two-degree cut. Reason is like a circular saw, in that the results it produces are also dependent on, for lack of a better term, the angle at which it is set. In the case of reason, the angle is the starting assumption or presupposition of the person using it. This is why, given the presuppositions or explicit beliefs it has to work with, reason can bring two different people pondering the same issue to two opposite and yet rationally consistent conclusions. The problem is not with reason as a tool, but with the presuppositions and beliefs that set the "angle" upon which reason will do its work.

What is it that sets the angle of reason? I'm persuaded that those who claim that reason is their authority have mistaken what philosophers call *intuition* for *reason* and then elevated their own intuition to their ultimate criterion of truth. Intuition is a mental state in which a claim simply seems true to the person confronted with it. For example, the proposition that "all men are created equal" probably seems true to you without argument or evidence. Many, if not most of, our beliefs can be traced back to intuition as their source and grounding. But the "seeming so" experience of intuition is not reason. Intuitions are beliefs that arise spontaneously within us, but that does not mean they are indicative of truth. There are many factors that influence our intuitions, ranging from our psychological makeup, our personal values, and our sociocultural settings, to name a few. For many individuals, it's their intuitions that set the "angle" of the saw of reason and, consequently, bring them to their conclusions.

Lest I be misunderstood, let me be clear. The problem isn't with reason as a tool or our ability to reason correctly—it's what standard we choose to reason according to. Even the most logical and intelligent thinkers will arrive at wrong conclusions if they are reasoning according to the wrong standard. And make no mistake, everyone has some ultimate authority that determines what the reasoning process will lead them to conclude is true. Thus, it's important to help believers see that, out of all the competing standards according to which reason can operate, it is the Bible that they should adopt.

Presuppositions. Believers need to understand that when it comes to choosing an ultimate criterion by which they are going to reason, that choice is fundamentally presuppositional in nature. Whatever one's ultimate authority is, that authority must use its own standards in proving its conclusions. This is easy to see. If I say, "X is true," and you ask why I believe that, and I say, "because Y is true," you will ask why I believe Y is true. This reason-giving process cannot go on forever. We cannot argue in an endless chain of reasons—otherwise, we would never establish our belief about X. So, to argue at all, we must assume the truth of something, and that something must be taken as self-evident. It must be a truth that we do not and cannot appeal to any other higher criterion of authority in order to justify it. If we do, then whatever that is becomes our authority.[2] In all arguments, we take for granted the authority of certain ideas, principles, or beliefs. Every ultimate authority or criterion must assume itself in order to be consistent. There is a degree of circularity here, but it's circularity that's inescapable. Those who appeal to reason as their ultimate criterion justify doing so *by using* reason. But if they appealed to anything else to justify reason, reason would not be their ultimate criterion. Therefore, every final authority is self-attesting. If this is the case, then can we ever decide between ultimate authorities to direct our reasoning if the choice is fundamentally presuppositional in nature and not the result of evidence?

Which presupposition? Whose authority? The answer lies in asking which fundamental presupposition is able to account for and provide meaning to the human experience on its own terms. This is done by reasoning according to the presupposed, ultimate authority and following it out to its logical conclusions. The Bible's claim is that it is a revelation from God. We do not reason from the ground up to God, but God has revealed himself to us. When we presuppose God's Word as our ultimate authority and follow it out to its logical conclusions, we find that it can account for the totality of the human experience we take for granted. For instance, the Bible provides the precondition for the intelligibility of the laws of logic, morality, maintaining our identity over time, the existence of universals, the uniformity of nature (which science requires), freedom, and dignity, to name just a few. Moreover, the Bible is the best explanation compared to the other options available. Some have gone so far as to argue that no other presupposed, ultimate authority possesses the resources to serve as the precondition

---

[2] Joe Boot, *Why I Still Believe* (Grand Rapids: Baker Books, 2006).

for intelligibility—not empiricism, not rationalism, and not any other religious revelation—only the Bible.[3]

Let me recap the argument. Reason needs content to reason about. To come to true conclusions, it must have true premises. We get those premises from various sources, but we accept or reject them according to whether they align with our ultimate authority. A human tendency is to elevate our own subjective and fallible intuitions to the level of ultimate authority and then call that reason. Doing so is wrong. Our intuitions are not a reliable criterion, let alone an ultimate one, nor is reason an authority. It's a tool. Only the Bible, because it's a revelation from God, can be trusted to play the role as the ultimate authority because it originates from God and, as such, is wholly true. Since all ultimate authorities must presuppose themselves, there exist no external criteria by which competing claims to authority can be evaluated. Therefore, in order to rationally choose the best criterion, we must ask which one can account for the various elements of the human experience. When we do this, it becomes apparent that only the Bible has the resources to do so. Believers need to understand this so they will not be deceived into thinking that the Bible must be brought into line with something they call "reason," because as soon as that happens, the game is all but lost.

A Better Story, a Fuller Gospel

Many former believers reveal that, prior to their deconversion, they possessed a reductionistic and, frankly, in my opinion, distorted understanding of the Bible's grand narrative. As one reads or listens to former Christians recount their understanding of the story line of Scripture, one cannot help but wonder if a reason they abandoned the faith is that the Bible, as they understood it, was not only uninspiring but also

---

[3] Those familiar with the presuppositional apologetics of Cornelius Van Til and his protégé, Greg Bahnsen, will recognize their influence here. Van Til and Bahnsen maintain that only the God of the Bible can provide the precondition of intelligibility to make sense out of any facet of human experience. For a detailed explanation of this argument, see Greg Bahnsen, *Vat Til's Apologetic: Readings and Analysis* (Phillipsburg, NJ: P & R Publishing, 1988).

unappealing. Among the more conservative evangelical and fundamentalist sectors of the church, there exist various versions of the biblical story that fail to do justice to the story God is telling. The result is a truncated narrative that lacks the existential punch that the authentic gospel packs.

Let me begin by illustrating what I mean from my own experience. I grew up with an understanding of the Bible that went something like this: God created people to worship him. People rebelled against God. God loved them so much that he sent Jesus to die so we all didn't have to go to hell. The point of our earthly existence is to decide where we want to spend eternity and, after we do so, to try and help others go to heaven as well. But we need to do so while keeping unspotted from the world. That's because the world is broken and perishing and will only detract us from serving Jesus with all its temptations and vices. Because the world is literally and rightly going to hell, there is almost no justification for investing one's time or treasure in it. Only those things done for Christ are of any lasting value. Although mundane things such as work, education, and other secular activities are necessary, they are not of any real importance. In the end, if one chooses Christ, they will get to live with him in heaven, a place beyond the sky, where the redeemed sing songs all day around God's throne.

That, in my opinion, is not the story line of the Bible. And thank goodness it isn't, because it's neither a life-giving nor life-affirming message. It neither inspires nor provides any real sense of meaning to anything other than a small area of human existence. There are better, and by that, I mean more faithful, ways of cashing out the story of the Bible and the purpose of life. And, by no mere coincidence, they turn out to be more inspiring and attractive narratives.

The central message of the Bible is the gospel. The word *gospel* means *good news*—therefore, the central message of the Bible is one of good news. The question is, what is the content of the good news? Typically, the way that deconverts understood the story of the Bible is similar to how I once understood it. Perhaps a better way of putting it is that they have misidentified the gospel with the message of salvation.

Scot McKnight, in his book *The King Jesus Gospel*, persuasively argues that the gospel is not reducible to the Four Spiritual Laws, the Romans Road, or any other attempt to define it in a way that focuses solely on the work of Christ and how that reconciles one to God. McKnight maintains that the gospel, or good news, is not merely what he calls the message of salvation. The message of salvation, according to McKnight, is what is typically identified with the gospel. But, says McKnight, the gospel is broader and more encompassing than the message of salvation. The gospel is the story of the kingship of Jesus, which goes all the way back to the Garden of Eden and culminates in the book of Revelation, where God dwells with his people. As McKnight and many others read the story, God created Adam and Eve in his image. That is, he made them moral, relational, volitional, rational, creative beings that he desires to be in relationship with. That relationship consisted of them reflecting his glory by working with him as his vice regents, ruling over his creation. God placed them in the Garden and gave them the command to have dominion over the earth and to subdue it. Contrary to how this sounds, the thrust of the command—which has become known as the cultural mandate—was to mine out all the latent potential that he had built into the creation and cultivate it. They were to image him by taking the raw material he had made and creating artifacts that would assist them in their responsibility to have dominion over creation.

This is an important aspect of the story of the Bible because it clearly shows that prior to the Fall, the mundane things of life were considered meaningful. As opposed to the way I understood the story; God didn't create the world as a place for people to live while they decided where they would spend eternity. He created it as a home for people and a place where he would meet with them, and they would worship him by doing the mundane things I thought of as necessary evils. Humans creating art, music, sculptures, competing in sports, and pursuing an education were all part of God's original intention. They were not byproducts of the Fall. This understanding infuses all of life with meaning. God desires the salvation of the lost, but prior to that, he desired the creation of culture. He still desires that today. Seeing the story of the Bible in this light takes all of the activities of life, which, on their own, do not have any real value, and makes them potentially invaluable acts of or avenues for worship. Not only does preaching have value—so does plumbing. It's not just the missionary who is doing something that has eternal value, but the Christian merchant as well. What a difference from my early understanding of the biblical narrative, in which only the explicitly spiritual mattered.

Not only does a more faithful understanding of the big story of the Bible fill all of life with meaning; it also redirects the central aspect of the Bible's story, what we refer to as the gospel, from a simplistic message of salvation to a robust story of God ultimately restoring all of creation to the peace he intended at the beginning prior to the Fall. According to this reading, the goal of the gospel isn't getting into an ethereal heaven after death but being a member of the kingdom of heaven and serving Jesus and others as the flourishing individual one was intended to be.

In the robust gospel of the kingdom, a disembodied heaven is not the final destination of God's people. Instead, it's a garden city where God dwells with his people, who engage in meaningful activities serving him and others. In the book of Revelation, we find that God will finally get what he desired in the book of Genesis. In the Garden, God and humans had an uninhibited relationship and personal interaction. They were to be fruitful and multiply and, by doing so, bring more individuals into the bliss that was an immediate relationship with the God of the universe. Yet, we know that is not how things turned out. Adam and Eve rebelled, and in doing so, they separated themselves and their progeny from God. They also lost the right to rule and reign as God's sub-sovereigns over his creation. Humanity fell under the wrath of God, and the community was shattered. However, Jesus was the second Adam in that he was the man whom God appointed to be his representative of a new humanity. In Christ, God was doing at least two things. First, he provided a representative upon which to build the new community that he always intended. Jesus refers to this community as a kingdom. The kingdom that he had come to establish was one that is characterized by the peace of God. It is the perfect balance of grace, truth, love, and justice.

Second, as both God and man, Jesus possesses the characteristics that make such a kingdom possible. As a human, he can serve as a representative before God of all other humans, and he can serve as head of the sub-sovereigns that God had always intended to rule his creation. As God, he guarantees that where Adam failed due to his frailty and susceptibility to sin, he will succeed. Thus, Jesus as the king of the kingdom invites all of humanity into his realm, where they will find their deepest longings for meaning and significance met. But there is a problem. Everyone, because of their sin, is disqualified from entering the kingdom. They're guilty rebels, cosmic traitors who stand under the condemnation of God. Here is where the truncated message of salvation I once understood to be the big story of the Bible enters the big story. The king, out of love for his people, willingly sacrifices himself on their behalf. Those who are willing to pledge to him their allegiance by recognizing his sacrifice on their behalf and trusting in his death and resurrection find forgiveness for their sins. They are then welcomed into his eternal kingdom, which is already breaking into the existing order and one day will arrive in its fullness. When it does, it's not an ethereal heaven that believers will live in, but a grand garden city where God finally dwells with his people, and they reflect him by doing what he called them to back in the Garden. In the meantime, the lives of Jesus's followers are characterized by an expectant hope for the future and an assurance that in the present, whatever they do, whether a garbage collector or a prime minister, contributes to the Lord and his kingdom. That truly is good news!

The above understanding of the biblical narrative, or something like it, is a much more faithful rendition of the big story the Bible is telling. And it needs to be the kind of telling that we teach young people, if for no other reason than everyone lives their life according to some master narrative, whether they realize it or not. Therefore, we do believers a disservice by not telling the story of God and his plan for humanity in all its grandeur. While truth is the ultimate reason why one should adopt a narrative to live by (not that the story is simply inspiring or beautiful), the fact that the story of the Bible is inspiring, beautiful, and life-affirming adds to its attraction. There is no more beautiful and attractive story in all the world than the story of the Bible. Therefore, we ought to be telling it in all its glory, and when we do, we will avoid setting up believers for a crisis of faith as they try to remain committed to a story that is not only unattractive but also distorted.

Credibility-Enhancing Displays

It should come as no surprise that parents play an immensely important role in the faith development of their children. Research has long demonstrated this to be the case. Both the sociology and psychology of religion have repeatedly shown that religious socialization by parents is a major determining factor both in whether or not children believe in supernatural agents and which of those agents they believe in.[4] The study of parents and faith retention falls under the larger theoretical framework of social learning. Social-learning frameworks highlight the role that models play in the transmission of beliefs and the adopting of behaviors—models are defined as those significant and influential persons in a child's life. Along with the tendency to adopt beliefs and behaviors from influential models, individuals tend to form biases toward certain individuals as models based on certain factors. Two of these factors are prestige and conformist biases. Prestige bias biases learners toward those whom they view as having high levels of social prestige. Conformist bias biases learners toward the most common beliefs within their group.[5]

In 2009, Joseph Henrich identified a third bias, which he labeled credibility-enhancing displays, or CREDS.[6] Basically, what Henrich

---

[4] Jonathan A. Lanman and Michael D. Buhrmester, "Religious Actions Speak Louder than Words: Exposure to Credibility-Enhancing Displays Predicts Theism," *Religion, Brain & Behavior* 7, no. 1 (2017): 44.

[5] Lanman and Buhrmester, "Religious Actions," 4.

[6] Joseph Henrich, "The Evolution of Costly Displays, Cooperation and Religion: Credibility Enhancing Displays and Their Implications for Cultural Evolution," *Evolution and Human Behavior* 30 (2009).

argued for and demonstrated is that CREDS—"actions that (a) are consistent with a model's professed beliefs, and (b) a model would be unlikely to perform if he believed something different from what he expressed symbolically"—significantly increased the likelihood that learners would adopt the beliefs of the model.[7] In other words, Henrich found that a strong correlation exists between children expressing belief in intangible entities, such as God, when important adults in their life behave in accordance with that belief. For example, praying to God, attending church, and telling children to pray indicate to children that adults actually believe in God. This can be especially powerful when adults exhibit CREDS that are costly to them. When an adult is willing to suffer for their beliefs financially, socially, or simply in terms of losing out on a perceived good, it communicates that they really do believe what they claim. Parents who live authentic Christian lives in front of their children have a much greater chance of their children retaining their Christian faith. It must be stressed that it's in the living out the beliefs where the transfer occurs. Merely professing to believe in God or Christianity is not sufficient to effectively pass on the faith. The talk must be accompanied by the walk. Henrich explains:

> Several studies compare the effect and interaction of models who preach generosity or selfishness ("one ought to donate . . .") and practice either generous or selfish giving. Preaching alone usually has little or no effect on giving. Children's behavior seems uninfluenced by preaching when these exhortations are inconsistent with the model's actions. However, when a model actually donates generously, the subjects donate more generously. Here, giving away tokens that one could use to exchange for toys is a CRED of one's commitment to the verbal claim that "one ought to donate."[8]

What this tells us is that living out one's faith commitments (i.e., exposing individuals to high levels of CREDS) is key to setting up children

---

[7] Henrich, "Evolution of Costly Displays," 258.
[8] Henrich, "Evolution of Costly Displays," 249.

for successful spiritual commitment. Conversely, Joseph Langston discovered that individuals lose their belief in God at younger ages when their religious parents talk the talk but don't walk the walk.[9]

Interested in discovering why persons become atheists, Langston and his colleagues studied the relationship between exposure to CREDS and change in religious beliefs, specifically from theism to atheism. In their study of more than five thousand respondents who had deconverted, they discovered that those who came from homes with low exposure to CREDS renounced their belief in God earlier than those who came from homes that were characterized by exposure to high levels of CREDS. It's important to remember, as the authors point out, that CREDS are only one factor in why some individuals maintain faith and why others abandon it. At the same time, however, the importance of living out a faith that one professes plays a significant role in faith transmission and retention. The more parents live in accordance with what they say they believe, the more likely it is that their children will adopt those beliefs as their own.

Appropriate Apologetics

On one hand, I am persuaded that apologetics plays a role in spiritual formation. The Bible never calls for a blind leap of faith. Faith, biblically speaking, is having sufficient reasons for a hope worth acting on. It's not believing in something you suspect is untrue or for which you have no reasons to believe. Nowhere will you find the Bible demanding that kind of faith. John ends his Gospel with the following claim: "Jesus performed many other signs in the presence of his disciples, which are not recorded in this book. But these are written that you may believe that Jesus is the Messiah, the Son of God, and that by believing you may have life in his name" (John 20:30–31). John recorded specific events in the life of Jesus so that his readers would have reason to believe that Jesus was who he claimed to be. Paul reasoned with the Jews from the

[9] Joseph Langston, Thomas J. Coleman III, and David Speed, "Predicting Age of Atheism: Credibility Enhancing Displays and Religious Importance, Choice, and Conflict in Family Upbringing," *Religion, Brain & Behavior* 10, no.1 (Jan. 2018).

Old Testament scriptures that Jesus was the prophesied messiah. Peter instructed his readers to live in such a way that it would cause others to inquire about the reasons they had for hope in the face of difficulties. Having reasons for belief is both biblical and psychologically necessary. It's nearly impossible to believe in a claim that one has no evidence for. One might hope a claim for which they have no good reason for accepting is true, but to believe in it means having a positive attitude toward the belief being true. Apologetics, or reasons confirming the claims of the Bible, can help us do that; so too can good theology.

On the other hand, apologetics should not be the foundation upon which our faith rests. Faith, like a table, should be supported by numerous legs. One should be personal experience, another should be the testimony and experience of others, a third should be relationships with other believers, and the fourth should be empirical evidence and philosophical reasons. I say that more is required to have a stable faith than intellectual reasons because too many former believers once identified as amateur apologists. Upon further investigation, it appears that for some, although they had intellectual reasons for their faith, it was not anchored in a personal experience of God. I am not saying that their commitment was only intellectual assent, but what I am saying is that they seem not to have cultivated a deep, personal attachment to God that could withstand their intellectual doubts. Their faith was a matter of believing and standing for the truth, but it lacked a personal fidelity to Jesus.

Nevertheless, having reasons that support one's faith is important, but perhaps more important is knowing the limitations of apologetics and what one can expect from reason. It seems that budding Christian apologists who became former Christians lacked this awareness. Furthermore, they also exhibited a sense of confusion about the nature of what it means to believe in Jesus. I am of the opinion that these two factors, a misunderstanding of what apologetics can do and a confusion about what it means to believe, are related.

I am persuaded that Christian authors and publishers of apologetic material have created an unrealistic and harmful expectation of what it means to believe and the efficacy of apologetics in bringing such belief about. Former believers who were heavily into apologetics reveal that they assumed a particular definition of what it means to "believe," and they depended on apologetics to provide them with it. And who could blame them? One needs only to glance at the titles lining the shelves of any Christian bookstore to see why. *Without a Doubt, Beyond a Reasonable Doubt,* and *Evidence That Demands a Verdict* give the impression that the case for Christianity is overwhelming. Yet, when they encountered counter-apologetics, their belief was undermined, and they concluded that they were no longer believers. Why is that? I think the reason lies in the confusion they had over what it means to be a believer.

Often, the Bible uses the English words *believe* and *faith* interchangeably. While there is a slight difference between the two, both words share the same root and indicate a range of meanings. But the primary meaning of both is to trust in someone or something. Consequently, what the Bible calls individuals to is to trust in the person and work of Jesus. In contemporary English, though, the word *belief* means something different. To believe is to have a positive attitude toward a particular truth claim that is based on reason and evidence. Therefore, the more positive one feels about a truth claim, the more they can be said to believe it. This naturally leads to the conclusion that being certain is the greatest level of belief one can have, and this is often what apologetics has promised to provide. But when former believers encountered atheist apologists who undermined their confidence, they concluded that they were no longer believers because they equated real belief with being certain, or at least nearly certain. Naturally, then, if, to be a believer, one has to be near certain of what they believe, former Christians equated their doubt as a sign they had lost their faith.

It's at least conceivable that if former believers, who depended so heavily on apologetics to underwrite their faith, had a more biblical understanding of both apologetics and faith, they could have avoided their crises. Biblically speaking, as mentioned above, to believe is not to have certainty or necessarily a high degree of psychological confidence.

Instead, it is to be persuaded enough that the claims of Christ are true that one adopts the Christian story as their own and lives under the lordship of Christ. This does not require certainty. It is, like every other kind of meaningful decision that one will make in life, fraught with a level of uncertainty. Believing in Jesus is more akin to entering into a marriage relationship than it is affirming the answer to a math equation. Despite having many good reasons that the person one is going to marry is a good choice, there will always be room for doubt. But if one waits until they are certain the person they're marrying is the right one, few people would ever get married. Being a Christian, like getting married, requires trust and commitment based on reasons. But the ability of those reasons to produce anything close to certainty in an individual has more to do with the psychological makeup of the individual than it does the nature of the reasons themselves.

Apologetics can provide reasons that can, in turn, instill confidence that Christianity is true. But it can never demonstrate that it is beyond all doubt. There are and always will be counterarguments that attempt to either rebut or undermine the claims of Christianity. At times, such claims can create doubt in the mind of a believer. But doubt is only a problem for a faith that equates belief with certainty or something similar. The opposite of faith is not doubt but certainty, which is ironic, given the assumptions of so many deconverts that true faith is nearly synonymous with certainty. Doubt, as opposed to being the opposite of faith, is a companion of faith. Faith can only exist where doubt is possible. If there were no room for doubt, we would not have to trust at all, and trust is the essence of biblical faith. Apologetics can provide reasons for hope, but faith is acting on that hope. The confidence one has in the reasons supporting the claims of the Bible will wax and wane, but as long as there are sufficient reasons to act, faith and doubt will coexist. Believers need to know that it's okay to doubt and question, and that being a believer is defined more as entering into a commitment to Jesus than being psychologically certain that the claims of the Bible are true. No doubt, a level of confidence in the Bible's claims must be present in order to do so. But that level need only be where the preponderance of the evidence is in favor of Christianity rather than the evidence that Christianity is true beyond a reasonable doubt.

I want to encourage those who are actively involved in discipling others or those who are in a position of leadership in the church to utilize apologetics, but to do so with wisdom. There are good reasons that can be offered that confirm the claims of the Bible. But apologetics alone is insufficient to provide a robust foundation for faith. It needs to be supplemented by one's own experience with God and the support that one receives from being in community with others who are experiencing God. When apologetics is called upon to shore up our mental assent, we remember that it's a limited and at times weak tool. It will never provide certainty, and, at best, it can only provide varying degrees of confidence. That's okay, because biblical faith does not require certainty—it only requires enough confidence to trust and act.

Four Factors of Faith Cultivation

Disasters occur in many cases because they were not averted when they could have been. While it's not always the case, many unfortunate events could have been avoided if certain steps were taken in advance or if certain initiatives were launched before it was too late. As I write this section, it's the day after the heartbreaking crash of the helicopter that was carrying Kobe Bryant and his thirteen-year-old daughter, Gigi, along with seven others to a basketball practice only about thirty miles from where I live. As more information becomes available, it's increasingly clear that the tragedy could have been avoided had different choices been made that day. But hindsight is twenty-twenty, and I'm not looking to place blame on anyone for what happened. Nevertheless, it's clear that had different decisions been made, the chopper would not have gone down in the hills overlooking Calabasas, California.

When it comes to the loss of faith, I'm persuaded of something similar. From a human perspective, there are things that we unintentionally do that contribute to an individual losing their faith. Therefore, we ought to do what we can in order to avoid and avert that kind of disaster. In the previous chapter, I identified what some of those things are.

In this chapter, I have attempted to say that it is not enough to simply avoid placing stumbling blocks in front of believers. We also ought to be doing all that we can to cultivate faith in them. We can do so by helping them see that reason, while a God-given gift to aid us in processing information, is not the ultimate criterion for truth. This is important because it's often a certain conception of reason (as in an objective ultimate criterion of truth) that tempts believers to substitute the Bible for it. I have also maintained that an important component of cultivating faith is the inspiring account of the biblical narrative. Additionally, I have maintained that credibility-enhancing behaviors be regular components of our lives. We need to not only talk the talk but walk the walk. Doing so adds a measure of authenticity and attractiveness to the faith we profess. Finally, I suggested that what I have called appropriate apologetics should be used to confirm the truths of the biblical narrative. By providing believers with evidence and reasons why the faith is true—without making the faith rest completely on the success of apologetics—we can give believers the tools they need to think critically about the challenges that will inevitably be leveled against their faith.

CHAPTER THIRTEEN

STORIES OF RETURN

Reconverts

Whoever said "You can never go home again" was wrong. Former believers can and do return to the faith they once abandoned. I believe it's important to hear their stories, if for no other reason than the fact that getting to the end of a book on deconversion can leave one feeling discouraged. But there are other reasons to include the stories of those whom I am calling *reconverts*. After speaking on this subject in various venues, I have become painfully aware that those who are the most interested in this subject are those who are the most affected by it. As a result, I have purposed to end all my talks with stories of those who have returned to their faith to provide hope to those whose hearts break for their prodigals. Therefore, I will finish this book with a brief look at three individuals who have survived the kinds of faith-shaking crises that more often than not end in permanent deconversion. I hope that, in doing so, it provides comfort that there is a difference between being a Judas and being a Peter. Despite both having denied Christ, only one was lost. In the case of Peter, his reconversion occurred quickly, but that is not always the case. What the following stories demonstrate is that this is not the norm. Reconverts have gone decades before returning.

Consequently, we should always continue in prayer on their behalf, with the expectant hope that God will grant them repentance.

Reasonably Speaking

Darrin was raised in Texas and grew up in a Christian environment. He prayed to received Christ and was baptized at the age of seven. He read the Bible, evangelized others, and, according to him, tried as hard as he could to live as a Christian. But over time, he came to the conclusion that he was being fed lies. The reason? He was convinced that the Bible taught that God chose some people to go to heaven and condemned others to hell, even before they were born. To him, God seemed like a grand puppet master creating humans for his own glory, even if it meant their eternal suffering. Wanting no part of such an unfair and capricious God, he left the faith.

In spite of the fact that he no longer was a Christian, Darrin had a deep interest in the philosophy of religion and theology. However, now he was looking at those subjects from the outside, as an atheist leaning agnostic. On the Internet, he found other individuals who, like him, enjoyed talking and writing about the shortcomings and falsehood of religion, particularly Christianity. Eventually, he found himself connected with a well-known website for former Christians—one that sought to debunk Christianity. Darrin became a regular contributor to the website and dedicated himself to demonstrating that Christianity was irrational and false. He did so for years. But then something happened. Darrin changed his mind. He posted the following message on his website:

> Sometime last week, I realized that I could no longer call myself a skeptic. After fifteen years away from Christianity, most of which was spent as an atheist with an active, busy intent on destroying the faith, I returned to a church (with a real intention of going for worship) last Sunday. Although I

know I may struggle with doubt for the rest of my life, my life as an atheist is over.[1]

He added:

> Briefly, I grew tired of the lack of explanation for: the existence of the universe, moral values and duties, objective human worth, consciousness and will, and many other topics. . . . I realized that I could not answer them no matter how many long nights I spent hitting the books.[2]

The Christianity that Darrin has returned to isn't the Christianity that he left. It's not the conservative, evangelical denomination he once attended, but it is one that is theologically orthodox. And that's okay. Because even though he might not be a Christian in the way that some would like him to be, he is now serving the Lord and allowing God to continue to mold him into the image of his Son.

Alternative Options

For almost a decade, Derek wrestled to understand how the message of the gospel positively impacted the world. He was raised in what sounds very much like the kind of fundamentalist church that acted as a causal factor in so many deconversions—one espousing that the purpose of Christianity was to convert people to the faith and then avoid temptations and keep separate from the world. As he grew up, it became increasingly difficult to make sense of how his church divided the world. His church saw reality as comprising two distinct spheres: the secular and the sacred. The secular was bad through and through, and those who identified with the sacred should keep themselves from being associated with the secular. But that way of thinking didn't make sense to

---

[1] James Bishop, "Darrin Rasberry's Journey from a Christ Hating Atheist to Christ Follower," *Bishop's Encyclopedia of Religion, Society and Philosophy* (blog), May 21, 2015.

[2] Bishop, "Darrin Rasberry's Journey."

Derek because he saw that bad things were happening in the church and among fellow Christians and that good things were occurring in the secular world and among unbelievers. He sought out answers for why, if the secular world was so bad, it was filled with so many good, beautiful, and even true elements, and why the Christian world contained so much bad. No one provided him with answers that made sense. By the end of high school, he had become so disillusioned with the version of Christianity he'd inherited that he was ready to leave Christianity behind.

Several years later, Derek became friends with a young woman who invited him to attend a church with a decidedly different outlook on how Christians should relate to the world. Instead of seeing the world as something to be retreated from, they saw it as a place where Christians should be involved and have a prominent role in the culture as redemptive agents on behalf of the gospel. Discovering that there was another way of being a Christian—a different flavor, perspective, outlook, call it what you like—was what saved him from apostasy. "I still remember the peace that I felt at that church and how her Christian family seemed so, well, normal," he said. "Getting to know them and seeing in them a whole different side of the Christian faith was a major turning point in my life."[3]

Years later, he enrolled in seminary to pursue a master's degree in theology. When he stepped onto campus his first day, he had a very basic understanding of what the Reformed theology and worldview was. The more he was exposed to the work of Calvin, Kuyper, and other Reformed thinkers, the more he saw how the Reformed approach filled in the missing pieces of his childhood faith.

What Derek found that filled in the gaps was a perspective that taught Christians should be engaging the world for Christ as his representatives in every legitimate field of endeavor. Christianity became relevant to every area of life, making even the most mundane activities meaningful if done as acts of worship to God. This was a much more

---

[3] Derek Atkins, "Finding Faith Again," Christian Reformed Church, March 4, 2014.

satisfying version of Christianity than what he'd been taught by his fundamentalist church, focused as they were on abstaining from sin and keeping unspotted from the world.

Recommitted to his faith, Derek had to think about how he would explain his new perspective on Christianity to his friends, both unbelieving and those he grew up in the church with. His original tradition emphasized not only separation from the world but also confrontational evangelism. No longer of that persuasion, he wanted to show his non-Christian friends that beautiful and thoughtful expressions of Christianity existed and that being a Christian didn't mean one had to be judgmental and condemning.

What saved Derek's faith? It was realizing that the Christianity he was reared in, one which he took to be pure, unadorned Christianity but one that he could not accept, was just one of a number of takes on the faith that were open to him. It was realizing that he could be a Christian in other ways. Discovering that being a Christian did not require him to flee the world but engage the world for Christ made all the difference. Derek said, "I've seen both the beauty and the pain of the world. I have a different view now and that helps shape my message about what God is doing in the world. Without God, nothing makes sense. That's what brought me back."[4]

Like Derek, believers need to know that while there are a number of essential beliefs that one must hold to be a Christian, there is a great variety of ways to be an orthodox Christian. Throughout the history of the church, believers of all stripes have lived faithful lives in line with the nonnegotiable doctrines of the faith, all the while disagreeing on secondary and tertiary doctrines and practices. It's important to expose believers to the broad spectrum of beliefs and practices that exist within the boundaries of historic orthodoxy. By doing so, we provide them with a flexible faith, one that is less susceptible to mistaking their church's take for being the only game in town.

---

[4] Atkins, "Finding Faith Again."

The Power of Love

Benjamin, like Darrin, became a Christian early in life, but the immorality he experienced at the highest levels of his church was so damaging that it shook his faith to its core. It came to light that his pastor had committed multiple acts of adultery, embezzled money, purchased lavish homes and vehicles for himself with the money, and used illegal drugs. It would be nearly a decade before he stepped back into church again of his own free will. He noted:

> For me (and probably most of us) there was a giant disconnect between the character of Jesus and the way his followers demanded you live. *I liked Jesus.* He seemed kind and compassionate and enjoyed associating with the people I associated with (the party crowd). However, I wasn't interested in being a "Christian" if it meant looking like the status quo. His people were moral Nazis, and they had really strange rules.[5]

What was it that brought Benjamin back to his faith? In a word, it was love. At age twenty-seven, he met two men who changed his view of what it meant to be a Christian. They were tattooed, loved beer, and didn't fit the mold of what a Christian was supposed to look like, according to his former church. In fact, they looked exactly the opposite. But it was how they lived that impacted Benjamin:

> What won me over was the way they loved me and loved people who were hurting and messy. It was the way they shared openly about their hurts and repeated failures. It was the way they loved their wives and spoke so highly about them. It was the joy they had even in the midst of tears and deep suffering. It was the fact they didn't pretend to have it all together or all the answers. Sometimes they would just say *"I don't know."*[6]

---

[5] Benjamin Sledge, "Why I'm a Christian (And Continue to Suck at Being One)," *HeartSupport* (blog), October 17, 2016, emphasis in original.

[6] Sledge, "Why I'm a Christian," emphasis in original.

Their honesty, love, and commitment to living out the message of Jesus were infectious. Benjamin saw in them something he wanted for himself. Rather than asking him to pray the sinner's prayer, however, they told him that following Jesus had a high cost. Jesus wasn't interested in coming into his heart. He wanted his life. And that is just what Benjamin gave him:

> What's funny is when I became a Christian, I never asked
> Jesus into my heart. I never went to the front of the church
> to let everyone know I was down with this whole confusing
> Jesus dies on a cross, resurrects, and is God, but God can't die
> because he's eternal. . . . Instead one day I had this epiphany
> that *"I'm all in and I guess I'm one of them."*[7]

And, all in he is. Today, Benjamin, the young man who once left Christianity with no desire to return, is a pastor. He is actively loving people into the kingdom by letting them know that no one is beyond God's grace. And, as one who previously renounced his faith, he knows that better than anyone.

Homeward Bound

I began this chapter by claiming that whoever said "you can't go home again" was wrong. Informed readers may know that the person who said that was the American author Thomas Wolfe. The well-known phrase is actually the title of one of Wolfe's posthumously published novels. However, there is a sense of irony in Wolfe's title that's related to an event in his own life. In 1929, Wolfe published the novel *Look Homeward, Angel*, which painted an unflattering picture of his hometown of Asheville, North Carolina. His portrayal of the residents, his family members, and friends enraged them. The true identities of his thinly veiled characters were easy to discern, leading many in Asheville to feel he had betrayed them by revealing their moral failings. For his part, Wolfe made no apologies for his depiction of the town. On the

---

[7] Sledge, "Why I'm a Christian," emphasis in original.

contrary, years later, he wrote that, despite having no intentions to go back, he often entertained imaginary arguments and debates he would have with those who would challenge his portrayal of them and the town if he ever were to go back.

And yet, seven years after publishing his inflammatory novel, he did, in fact, go home again. Wolfe returned to Asheville in 1936 for a short visit. While there, Wolfe was asked by the editor of the local newspaper to write an article that would, in some respects, help restore his public image. It's clear from Wolfe's article, which he simply titled "Return," that he realized that, indeed, in one sense, a person can return home again. The end of Wolfe's article summarizes the common journey of those who strike out on their own to make their mark in the world as one characterized, first of all, by a "flight" from home on a "quest" to find significance, leading to "wandering" and then to a sense of "exile." But that is not where Wolfe leaves the journey. On the contrary, the journey ends not with exile and alienation, but with return. In fact, "return" is the final word of the article.[8]

Returning to the faith is a bit like the experience of Thomas Wolfe. It's a journey that can take a long time, is characterized by a flight from the faith in a quest for truth, that for many leads to a sense of wandering and exile. But some, like Wolfe, do end the journey by returning "home" to the faith again. But in another sense, there is some truth in Wolfe's famous saying that "you can't go home again." That is, because as Wolfe found when he returned home, it looked somewhat different to him than when he left. Things had changed in how he saw the town, and things had changed within him as well. Such will be the case for those who have left the faith but complete the journey and return home again. In most cases, the faith that they rediscover will, like Wolfe's view of Asheville, look somewhat different than the faith they left. It may be leaner in essential beliefs or perhaps more open to thinking about matters of faith from alternative perspectives. Nevertheless, those who wrestle with their faith, flee, and return are often rewarded with a

---

[8] Dale Neal, "Read What Wolfe Said to Asheville in 1937," *Citizen Times*, May 18, 2016.

stronger, more stable faith in the end—a faith that, for the first time, is their own and one they hold with a greater sense of personal commitment. Being mindful of this is crucial for those walking with a loved one who is in the throes of a faith crisis. God can and does continue to woo deconverts to return to him again, prodding and leading them home again, where he is waiting to receive them with joy.

AFTERWORD

In the five years since I began interviewing former believers, not all have remained former believers. At least one very unlikely individual has returned to faith. Lauren kindly shares the rest of her story to remind and encourage us that not all who wander are lost.

~

I returned to faith while on my knees, my body crumbled up in a towel, tears dripping on my faux wood floor. Hysterically sobbing, I managed to get out three words in between ragged breaths: *Jesus, help me.* Words barely audible to the naked ear were like a thunderous boom to God, who not only heard my plea but also felt my anguish. In that moment, he rejoiced and welcomed his prodigal daughter home after being away for more than a decade.

My deconversion was the result of being as excommunicated as one can be from an Evangelical church. After leaving the church, I became agnostic for a few years until I enrolled in graduate school to study sociology. A desire to research deviant and stigmatized populations led me to study nonbelievers. My own research on deconversion, consistent with the findings in this book, caused me to champion for nonbelieving underdogs. I became a secular activist within the national atheist movement in the United States, approaching life from a Humanist perspective while intentionally adopting a strong atheist identity. I gave talks, published papers, and worked on multimillion-dollar national campaigns, all in the name of atheism and ending secular discrimination.

I did not realize it at the time, but as a secular activist, God was not far from me. I retained a total of three strong Christian friends from my former Christian life, two of whom were a married couple working in ministry who left my previous church before I did. They spent many years unlearning legalistic tendencies and rigid adherence to Scripture. They learned how to love people where they are, without condemnation and judgment. They prayed for God to work in my life, which he did through them. They allowed me into their home and around their children. They offered to pray for me (which I always accepted) without trying to reconvert me. They loved and accepted me while remaining true to their convictions. In short, they showed me a different kind of Christian.

They say there comes a point in the life of an addict where they hit rock bottom, and it is only at this point that recovery can begin. I believe this to be true for deconverts as well. As stated in this book, there are several factors and well-reasoned arguments that lead and keep people away from their faith. But there are just as many reasons to return to faith. I was an out and out atheist activist and scholar and arguably the least likely to return to a place of belief—but I did return. The catalyst for my return was the momentary death of my daughter resulting from a heroin overdose; and in that moment, when I could not get up off the floor, I prayed. I considered the impact regaining faith would have on my career and my relationships, and I prayed anyway. I prayed because I needed a miracle. I prayed because I realized my anger was not with God. I prayed because I learned that I could follow Jesus differently than I had been taught. I prayed, and God answered. My reconversion was the result of a traumatic event, but regaining faith does not need to be wrought with trauma or despair. It does, however, require love. In his letter to the church at Corinth, Paul wrote, "And now these three remain: faith, hope and love. But the greatest of these is love" (1 Cor. 13:13). If there is someone in your life who has lost their faith, I encourage you to have hope and just love them. It was trauma that brought me to my knees, but it was love that brought me back to God.